# PURPOSE AND PRAISE

*If we once accept the premise that we can build a better world by using the different gifts of each sex, we shall have two kinds of freedom; freedom to use untapped gifts of each sex, and freedom to admit freely and cultivate in each sex their special superiorities.*
Margaret Mead, Anthropologist.

*Equal partnership between the female and male halves of humanity is key to a more just and peaceful world.*
Riane Eisler, The Center for Partnership Studies

*We have a huge opportunity to influence the future course of humanity through mate choice by being aware of the dynamics of sexual selection.*

*[Lysistrata's] strategy would have worked equally well over evolutionary time: female sexual preferences for peace-keepers could have reduced male belligerence and aggressiveness.*

*Today, evolutionary biology is proclaiming that the old map of evolution was wrong. It put too much weight on the survival of the fittest and, until the 1980s, virtually ignored sexual selection through mate choice.*
Geoffrey Miller, Ph.D., Evolutionary Psychologist.

*Using the Darwinian claim that it is the females in a species who choose their male mates, ... Donna Oehm Sheehan and Paul Reffell promise that seduction led by women can be passionate, playful, joyous, and most of all, effective and justified,*

*indeed virtually mandated by biological precedent among primates. They advocate relationships initiated on this vision of gender equality as a microcosm of what could become a template for egalitarian partnership throughout society.*
Margaret Mackenzie, Ph.D., Anthropologist

*Picking up from Darwin's theory of Sexual Selection, Seduction Redefined is an audacious and evocative look at male and female sexuality and the mating game. The premise of women as being in the evolutionary drivers seat will undoubtedly have huge implications for generations to come. A definite "must read.".*
Lesley Osman, M.A., M.F.T., Eco-Therapist, www.ecoroots.org

*Seduction Redefined ... seems a breath of relief for women residing in the United States. Contrary to "The Rules" of the mid-1990s, from this approach women are informed that they can take the driver's seat, be flirtatious and assertive, and still win that prized mate.*
Rosemarie Sokol, Ph.D., Social Psychologist

*Not another book on gender issues? Yes, and a necessary one it is! Finally, a fresh and fascinating look at exactly what is going on inside us when men and women get together.*
John Scherer, Author of *Work and the Human Spirit*.

*Paul, what you've written should be taken to heart by many men. It's humorous and easy to take, but nevertheless fosters an important attitude adjustment for men who wonder why they're alone. From time to time, I have male clients who can use this advice and I want a copy on hand for them.*
Larry Starr-Karlin, J.D., M.F.T. Psychotherapist

*Seduction Redefined... leaps to the forefront of a new movement in science and feminism that gives young women (and old) permission to return to the wisdom of their ancestral sisters and make them aware that their gender most likely was responsible for how our species was formed, and, more importantly, to decide the direction our species will be heading in the future; it shouts out, that, without this power, our species most likely will be doomed to extinction because of economic and environmental greed.*
William Spriggs, www.evoyage.com

*Bravo to your good work.*
Helen Fisher, Ph.D., Anthropologist, Chemistry.com science advisor

*This book will lead its reader on a path of truths that have always been there, just never really understood, or have even been hushed.*
Dorothy Lafrinere, womensselfesteem.com

# Praise and Purpose

*To me, Darwinian feminism is, first of all, a feminism that is prepared to investigate the growing body of knowledge from the biological and evolutionary sciences regarding evolved psychosexual differences between women and men. It is a feminism that would take these evolved differences into account and that would strive for a world in which the interests of both sexes would be taken seriously.*

*Second, a Darwinian feminism would use knowledge about our evolved dispositions to strive for a more just and more peaceful world. It would look for strategies to "work around" less palatable components of human nature, by seizing upon some of our more constructive evolved dispositions.*
 Griet Vandermassen, Ph.D., Evolutionary Psychologist

*Donna Sheehan, who left her work as an artist to battle against toxins in California, has gone on to apply her creative imagination to fostering peace. Always outrageous, she's now written a modern-day twist on* Lysistrata*. Her book,* Seduction Redefined, *urges women to take the lead by using the power of love to keep the peace.*

Ann Medlock, The Giraffe Heroes Project. www.giraffe.org

# Seduction REDEFINED

A GUIDE TO CREATIVE COLLABORATION OF
THE FEMININE & MASCULINE

BY

DONNA OEHM SHEEHAN AND PAUL REFFELL

© 2011 Donna Oehm Sheehan and Paul Reffell

All Rights Reserved

www.SeductionRedefined.com
info@SeductionRedefined.com

Published in the U.S.A. by Pioneer Imprints
P.O. Box 600, Ross, CA 94957

PIØNEER
IMPRINTS

Cover art by Deutsch Design Works
www.ddw.com

ISBN 978-0-9818318-7-9

# PREFACE

*There are only two problems on the planet – Men and Women!* This is more than just a bumper sticker. It's a wake-up call to get us thinking of ourselves as a species that needs the innate strengths of BOTH its sexes IN TRUE PARTNERSHIP to survive and to nurture the planet that supports it. That's where Seduction – redefined as a natural influence for good – comes in.

Our large brain has given us the ability to imagine and create, as well as hate and destroy. We have been a successful species of social animals that form families, tribes and cultures. We have also conjured up the concept of war against our fellow humans and justifications for it. Our brains have given us the hubris to think that we can somehow survive when we drive other species to extinction and poison the air, water and land that support us.

And what does all this doom and gloom have to do with seduction? Hang on!

It would be easy to say that all these problems are created by men, but women share the responsibility by encouraging, or not sufficiently discouraging, destructive male behavior of the men in their lives. And, perhaps most importantly, by selecting men with destructive habits as mates.

There's no blame here, because at this stage in our evolution, we are all products of the cultures in which we live. They are artificial constructs originally meant to support us, but have been so biased towards men for so long that something as basic as choosing a suitable mate has also become an unnatural process and seduction has been denigrated by male culture.

For example, the male-dominated film and advertising industries survive on the titillation of our basic drives by offering myths and products that purport to illustrate and satisfy them. That in turn perpetuates the need for those myths and products. The misinformation and the distortion of seduction for profit only complicate relations and cause misunderstandings between the sexes.

A quick review of my own life revealed a history of uneven experiences with men – based on my biological fascination with their bodies, my fear of the unknown, my low self-esteem, unrealistic expectations (like being swept off my feet by my Knight in Shining Armor), and going along with the popular convention of sarcasm in conversation with men. These were cultural norms, and I hold accountable the culture I inhabit for my living alone for years and for damaging the men around me. And it's still happening in every generation.

Most men do not want nor have the ability to be 'Knights in Shining Armor'. They want to *display* how suitable they are for mating, preferably without *appearing* to be displaying. They want to feel safe and loved in the arms of an understanding partner. They want understanding and kindness.

Women also want kindness from their mates. They also expect the Man Of Their Dreams to approach them, pursue them, to be the ready-made, perfect lover, husband, and father to their children. It's a recipe for disappointment. Statistics show high divorce rates, women resentful of men, and forty per cent of American children being raised by single parents. One study showed that American women are unhappy with their lives, marriages, children and work.[1] I think that women rediscovering their seductive potential can change that by forming true partnerships with men in all aspects of their lives.

Luckily for me, my intuitive seduction of Paul was the genesis of our partnership research and thus our discovery of Charles Darwin's theory of Sexual Selection. We realized what the rest of the animal kingdom has been showing us forever – women are responsible for their own romance and choice of partnership.

Once we began to understand the roots of human behavior in evolutionary terms, we applied it to the genesis of war. The first spark of *Seduction Redefined* was ignited by the global (mostly-male) media when they wrote about and published photographs of thousands of (mostly) women in naked protests inspired by our pro-peace organization, BaringWitness.org.

Baring Witness happened when I had a dream in 2002, provoked by the news of the impending invasion of Iraq, of women's bodies on the ground spelling PEACE. The male media treated Baring Witness with respect, however grudgingly, displaying a reaction to our vulnerability, lying nude and helpless on the earth. This global movement was a great revelation that vulnerability could be powerful and, yes, seductive! Thus, the gentle art of Seduction became a political word for us.

This science-based book will clear up most of your misunderstandings of the opposite sex. If taken to heart, it will lead

---

[1] A study released by the U.S. National Bureau of Economics and the University of Pennsylvania found that women are unhappier than they have been in 35 years, despite gains made in education and their place in the work force. http://bpp.wharton.upenn.edu/betseys/papers/Paradox_of_declining_female_happiness.pdf

to women learning to take responsibility for romance, women no longer waiting longingly for The Call, women remembering and regaining their biological feminine power in partnership with men.

Once women guide men into more conscious behaviors and into the equal brain partnership that our species really needs to survive, we just might save ourselves and our planet from men's unconscious displays of prowess.

Paul and I have written this book together, and you will see that the chapters have our names, either one or both, on each of them, to show from whose perspective they are written.

We use terms throughout the book that need explanation, so we placed the **Definitions** chapter at the beginning of the text. Feel free to skip the Definitions and dive into the first chapter on page 25.

Love, Partnership and Peace,  Donna Oehm Sheehan

# EDITOR'S FOREWORD
## Eve's Agenda

It's pretty audacious for Donna and Paul to put a picture of Eve and the Apple on the front cover of a book about genetic evolution, and about how great and important seduction is while referencing a religious tradition, but knowing them well enough by now I'm not surprised that they have once again playfully combined into one compelling meme, a deep taboo and a very, very good point.

So, in this spirit, we'll ask a simple question. Who made the first move, ever? At least according to Genesis, it was a woman. Eve to Adam.

This is definitely not a book about The Book, but the poetic images of myth can express the wisdom of life in a way that reaches our innate intuition. So I'm going to pick up and turn over a few familiar stones of a story that we all know so well, there in the Garden of Eden, to see if we really knew it after all.

This is not supposed to be revisionist, but more like the rest of this book, an attempt at getting a clearer picture of something familiar by removing some our inherited biases and assumption. By removing a lens we didn't even know we were wearing. The exercise will also get you used to this book presenting other familiar things, around courtship, mating, and the purpose of partnership, in a whole new light.

Please, if you need to swap out the clothes of these archetypes, in order to make this story more your own, feel free.

Let's begin with one of our culture's most insidious and unexamined beliefs. The kind that takes control of your perspective when you don't even realize it has. Like when you saw the front cover of this book.

That belief is that Eve got us all into this mess. That it's her fault we ate the Apple, which was the most bad thing ever. Understandably, believing this, we have been punishing her for it ever since. Whose fault was it really?

In those short, terse lines of Genesis, and it's really only a few dozen, God asks what happened. In brief, Adam passes the buck to Eve, Eve passes the buck to the serpent, God agrees with Eve, and the serpent gets cursed by God.

No divine principle curses Eve and Adam. It just levies the natural consequences of eating the red pill, and without blame. Almost like, "O.K. so if that's what you want, here's the deal, and here you go." In the original Hebrew there is nothing implying any emotional tone. God is not forcefully blaming or even reprimanding Eve.

But Adam (us guys), it appears, blamed (and still blame) Eve. The blame on women for "original sin" is so deep and unexamined that it has throughout history even been popular to portray the Eden serpent with breasts. So it wasn't just Eve, but meta-female herself. That bad, seductive female.

But really what was Eve's motivation? What in Heaven's name was she thinking? Was she weak willed, or did she make an instinctual choice (she had no knowledge of good and evil then) with her eyes wide open? Most people these days, if you ask, say without a

## Foreword

thought that Eve was overpowered by temptation. Women are the weaker sex after all, right?

Though she knew the potential consequences, Eve still made the decision to go ahead with eating the fruit. Then she somehow convinced/seduced Adam to join her, that all the pain they might go through would be worth it in the end.

They are expelled from Eden, and they land in the best school that we know of for learning of "Good" and "Evil", and of their fruits of "Pleasure" and "Pain". That school is our World.

It's common to see pictures of Adam and Eve weeping as they leave the Garden, in overwhelming regret. That too, like the blame on Eve, is an erroneous imputation, it's not in the story.

If we are to take this story as a mythic guide on its own terms, it's clear that living outside of the paradisiacal Eden has allowed Adam and Eve and their progeny to grow spiritually. It's hard, yes. But Eve seduced Adam into joining her in the decision to grow beyond their own ignorance. This is the key.

Is all this pain worth it? Are we to thank Eve for the Apple? Is it bitter? Sweet? Bittersweet?

Many women I speak with seem to instinctively think it is all worth it. Most men seem to be not so sure. And this is telling. But taken to its conclusion, the main loss in the Eden story, Adam and Eve's access to the fruits of the Tree of Life, is resolved in the end of Revelations when humans choose Good after gaining knowledge of the two options. When they're ripened enough.

Through the experiment and its travails we humans lift our status out of blissful ignorance and grow beyond ourselves. To, in the words of The Book, become as God.

Thanks, Eve.

## Challenge #1: Trusting Eve's agenda

According to the story, this all only is good in the end if we meet the challenge - otherwise it's all for naught. And the first challenge is the Big One. Adam still seems to be stuck on it: It's the choice of how to perceive Eve.

Was she actually acting, deliberately, with a deep instinct? Or was she swayed by temptation? This is important: our entire relationship to the female, and our ability to accept her initiating intuition as a trustworthy guide, depends on this one perceptual choice.

I've decided to take a leap of faith and assume that Eve did know what she was doing. Believe me, I have fought that one for a long time, and it turns out that's a pretty common attitude for men. The last thing a certain part of me wants to do is come down to earth with a woman and meet her in the nitty-gritty and flesh and blood of human life. To accept her smells on their mysterious terms; to risk that I may even delight in them.

I was for years one of the most extreme cases of Solo Man on a Mission, jetting around the world with just a bag, and you can ask my past girlfriends: I was quite impossible to corner, at least for long. Incorporating the dominant mythos of my culture as my spiritual compass, in truth I treated the seduction of females, or the pull to earth of my own inner female, as the very obstacle I needed to overcome.

I saw Eve as weak, not wise. She, after all, was the initiator of "The Great Mistake" who was just oblivious that it even was a mistake. She was so far gone that it wasn't even worth speaking with her about it, she'd never understand.

But now when Eve hands me the Apple, I'm much more trusting. I have less suspicion. Why?

Something in me changed at some point - maybe it was the profound joy of the children in my life, or realizing that my creative energy was exponentiated by a healthy-minded female. Maybe because I choose to see that brightness in her eyes as honest, not some trick of a carnivorous plant. Or that I've lived quite fully so many solo wandering years that I'm ready. Maybe it's that a cherished and respected female's style of loving, both in its nurturing and its deep passion, resembles something I equate with a divine principle. Or maybe it's just that I'm hardwired to find her simply irresistible, and I've given up fighting it - on the road to working with it.

Maybe it's the perfect setup for a good reason.

## Knowledge; who needs Knowledge anyways?

If it was Knowledge that Eve was after, and seduced us men into, I'm willing to risk laying down my halberd and meet the possibility that this is still going on. That she still is driven, by her nature and divine commission, to seduce men into Knowledge.

I am willing to do this because it appears that she may be acting in alignment with my own goals, albeit from another angle I can't understand on my own. I have come to believe that she can seduce us into exactly the kind of knowledge that is required to save this world and bring us as a species into harmony with the rest of the planet. The knowledge of differentiating between what is life supporting, and what is life destroying. The knowledge of Good and Evil. You know, the kind of knowledge that many men have quite obviously ignored - for a long time, by the looks of the planet under their watch - as a matter of tradition.

It is no surprise to me that men have used every trick in the book and every power play possible to keep themselves from feeling that they need to listen to woman's message of knowledge. That acknowledgment alone would require men to change themselves.

By simply making women wrong, for millennia, we can justify not listening, and thus not doing, the inner work. I'm not surprised, because I have a man's mind and I know how it operates.

I currently believe that it's partly because, despite our innate hero's call to courage, men hesitate to truly feel the fullness of reality. That it's scary to feel the knowledge of Good and Evil; we're daunted by the responsibility and even the rewards of living up to its standards. Also, I sense that many of us men are very uncomfortable with our own innate completeness, uncomfortable with the idea that we are in truth part female.

## Adam, Androgen, and the Inner Androgyne

Adam's rib aside, at least biologically speaking men come from women, and not just in birth. A human fetus always begins its life as a 'female'. It becomes a male due to the presence of the hormone androgen, regulated by the presence of a "Y" chromosome given by the father; a chromosome which the female can't give. But at that sex crossroads, it is not a choice of androgen or estrogen that makes a fetus 'female'. It's a choice of adding androgen, or just carrying on with what's there.

Yes men, I'm sorry to break it to you, that no matter how tough you are, you are in a sense a female + androgen, which we call 'male'. 'Female' is in fact the biological base template of a human being.

In Jungian terms, there is a corollary to this in our minds, and these female qualities of our psyche are called our Anima. The male qualities, the Animus. We all have both. Just like the debatably androgynous God of the Bible.

Michael Meade, the gifted mythologist shared some words about the Anima from which we might divine Eve's agenda, and her modus operandi : "Anima is an old name for Soul. Because Soul tends to have a feminine tone. Anima has issues. Anima is trying to intrigue us into the important issues in our life. Soul is not looking for simple comfort. It is looking for a complicated way of being deeply touched and moved by the world. And the Soul will get us into trouble in order to get us to change. The changes that are going on now, and the great troubles of the world, from the point of view of the Soul, are here to help us transform, and become ourselves. Because that's our only real job in this world. To allow our own soul to lead us into the transformation, and at the end be more fully ourselves, a more descended human and more complete person, able to act in concert with cultural imagination and with the cycling and flow of nature."

If this is Eve's agenda, I feel it's due that we give her, at long last, a chance to lead us where it's her place to lead. It may even be crucial to our survival.

This is, in the end, her experiment after all.

Shall we take a bite?


Alden Bevington
Editor - In - Chief
Pioneer Imprints

# ACKNOWLEDGMENTS

In the course of writing *Seduction Redefined*, we have spoken with thousands of thoughtful, eloquent, intelligent and generous people. Many of them are scientists, doctors and academics who qualify as authorities on the subjects contained in this book. Others are simply authorities on their own lives, and no less enlightening. Wherever we have been in the past few years, we have talked about the subjects in this book with almost everyone we meet, and they have responded with excitement and encouragement, for which we are deeply grateful.

Our special appreciation goes to Geoffrey Miller, Ph.D., evolutionary psychologist and author of *The Mating Mind*, the extraordinary book that introduced us to Darwin's theory of sexual selection. His clear and courageous study of the evolution of human nature through sexual choice opened our eyes to the need for a redefinition of seduction.

Thank you to Deutsch Design Works for the stunning artwork. And a big thank you to Alden Bevington of Pioneer Imprints for his editing, advice, foreword and for publishing this book.

*I dedicate and entrust the story of my life outside the box to the only man that could turn the box inside out and right side up – my beloved wordsmith and life partner, Paul.*     Donna Oehm Sheehan

# TABLE OF CONTENTS

PURPOSE AND PRAISE ................................................................................. i

PREFACE ...................................................................................................... vii

EDITOR'S FOREWORD ............................................................................... xi
    Eve's Agenda

ACKNOWLEDGMENTS ............................................................................. xix

INTRODUCTION ............................................................................................ 1

DEFINITIONS ................................................................................................. 5
    Donna & Paul: Understanding Each Other

CHAPTER ONE ............................................................................................. 25
    Donna: Seduction
    *Stepping into Power as the Feminine Seductress*

CHAPTER TWO ............................................................................................ 39
    Paul: Seduction
    *Receiving the Gift of Feminine Seduction*

CHAPTER THREE ........................................................................................ 49
    Donna: Selection
    *Ladies' Choice – Women Seeking and Selecting*

CHAPTER FOUR ........................................................................................... 59
    Paul: Selection
    *Men Display and Women Select*

CHAPTER FIVE ..................................................................................... 69
   Donna: Initiating
   *Women Initiating – Overcoming Fear*

CHAPTER SIX ........................................................................................ 87
   Paul: Initiating
   *Understanding Men's Insecurity*

CHAPTER SEVEN ................................................................................ 95
   Donna: Seducing
   *The How-to of Intricate Seduction*

CHAPTER EIGHT ............................................................................... 109
   Paul: Being Seduced
   *Seduction from a Male Perspective*

CHAPTER NINE .................................................................................. 119
   Donna & Paul: Seduction Hazards
   *Overcoming His Fight or Flight Mode*

CHAPTER TEN .................................................................................... 129
   Donna: From Lust to Love
   *Progressing From Eros to Agape*

CHAPTER ELEVEN ............................................................................ 143
   Paul: From Lust to Love
   *The Rake's Progress to Partnership*

CHAPTER TWELVE ........................................................................... 157
   Donna & Paul: Partnership
   *Personal Pointers*

CHAPTER THIRTEEN ...................................................................... 181
   Donna & Paul: Questions of Sex
   *Sensuality and the Redefining Woman*

CHAPTER FOURTEEN ..................................................................... 191
   Donna & Paul: The Brain Science
   *Two Brains of One Mind*

EPILOGUE ............................................................................................ 201
   Donna & Paul: Small Steps to Evolutionary Change
   *Where Do We Go from Here?*

ABOUT THE AUTHORS .................................................................. 215

INDEX .................................................................................................... 219

Sexual Selection
*Does every male of the same species excite and attract the female equally? Or does she exert a choice, and prefer certain males? This latter question can be answered in the affirmative by much direct and indirect evidence.*

Charles Darwin.
*The Descent of Man, and Selection in Relation to Sex.*
First published in 1871.

**se•duc•tion:** *noun:*

***1.*** something that entices or influences by attraction or charm.
(*Webster's Third New International Dictionary*)

***2.*** the ultimate Feminine agent of culture change.
(*Donna & Paul*)

# INTRODUCTION

*Seduction Redefined* asks women to awaken the power they all possess – the seductive power of the Feminine. It has been both deified and denied, because it is a force for change, and change is scary. But it is still there, in every woman, awaiting the awakening.

Donna's power awoke one night, and her intuitive inspiration to seduce Paul began the continuing journey of forming and sustaining a loving partnership. You'll read about the entire process from each of our separate points of view, as the seducer and the seduced, and from our conjoined view as long-term partners.

We want women and men to redefine the notion of seduction, to think of it as a natural, biological means of forming partnerships that have a chance. Forget everything you know about seduction and join us in freeing it from the taboo and acknowledging its scientific and evolutionary importance.

*Seduction Redefined* will help you to recognize the necessity of combining the best traits of the Feminine and Masculine in every part of our lives, especially our relationships. It will help women and men understand the evolutionary biology that makes seduction the most natural and effective source of change that we possess.

When we found out about Charles Darwin's theory of Sexual Selection, and the relatively new branch of study called Evolutionary Psychology, we understood that Donna's intuitive use of her biological power to select and seduce the mate of her choice was completely natural. And we saw that women's ability to guide men into true partnership is the foundation for forming stable, co-creative cultures in which the Feminine and the Masculine use their separate, complementary skills in unison, rather than in competition and with unrealistic expectations of each other.

We believe that humans have become the victims of their own males' mating displays. We think that women, or the Feminine essence in all of us, are the keys to changing those displays by making it obvious that such traits are less desirable than men believe them to be. That means women making conscious selections of their mates, and women guiding the men in their lives towards less destructive behavior, with kindness, love, understanding and no blame.

All change requires moving out of one comfort zone and forming another comfort zone. In this case, it's dedicating yourself to your own happiness, that of your partner and of those around you. It's about listening deeply, forgiving and recognizing our differences, understanding the brain science that explains them, and getting on with the business of making the human race live to its fullest potential.

If you're looking for true partnership, whether you're single or in a relationship, this book can help you. Women and men, including many in long-term relationships, are having a hard time understanding one another. The unfortunate result is the well known 'blame game'.

# Introduction

Women's and men's brains are built differently; they think and react differently; women express emotions more freely; men tend to be more motivated by sensual love, women by romantic love; men prefer to avoid confrontation in the home and look for ways to fix problems, and women think their men are being unloving and indifferent to their issues by not wanting to discuss them.

The gender of the brain, dependent as it is on hormonal influences in the womb, is on a continuum from Feminine to Masculine, which influences the usage of the structures that differ between the sexes.

*Seduction Redefined* gives you the information, inspiration and motivation you need to see past the misunderstandings to the new paradigm of true, loving partnership.

Examples of partnerships, romantic and creative, resonate down through the centuries and inspire others with their love and artistry. From the legend of Orpheus and Eurydice to John Lennon and Yoko Ono; from Shah Jahan, who built the Taj Mahal in memory of his beloved Mumtaz Mahal, through Abigail and John Adams and Dolley and James Madison to Rosalynn and Jimmy Carter; from Elizabeth Barrett and Robert Browning to Christopher Isherwood and Don Bachardy and Paul and Jane Bowles.

All could be described as partnerships of the Feminine and Masculine principles and their co-creative energy.

This book is written with heterosexuals mostly in mind, but we think the underlying principle, of re-empowering the Functional Feminine and Masculine within all of us, applies universally to all human beings, whether androsexual, gynosexual, bisexual or transgender. So this book is for all of us, and we hope it will inspire readers to pay attention to their Functional energies.

*Seduction Redefined* can get us all started on the road to a revolution in gender equality, a partnership society in which women and men work together at home, in business and in government to complement the best of both the Feminine and Masculine energies and brain differences. Enjoy the journey!

# DEFINITIONS
## Donna & Paul: Understanding Each Other

*Female choice is a fundamental, important process that shapes organic evolution.* Geoffrey Miller, Ph.D.[2]

In this book we use terms such as sexual selection, Alpha, Alpha-Mask, Beta, etc. Here are some definitions and basic information, so that we will all be able to understand each other.

We have placed this section before the first chapter for easy reference, but **feel free to go straight to the main text, beginning on page 25**, and return here later for clarification.

Part of our intention with this book is to help readers to view the human race as just another animal species. In that vision, we can study ourselves with a certain detachment that does not allow the hubris that holds us above Nature. We can analyze our behaviors, the structure of our cultures and our mating habits.

---

[2] From an interview recorded for our documentary film on Sex, War and Seduction, which is still in production. www.BaringWitnessFilm.org

## Evolutionary Behaviorism – Display

**1.** Most human inventions and male behaviors, including literature, music, art, invention, exploration, technology, aggression, altruism, complicated language and shows of physical strength, stem from male mating displays to attract the female.

**2.** Females of most species actively select male mates based on the males' displays. Males compete with other males for female attention, but do not actually select their mates. They respond to the proximity of a female that is ready to mate and that may be giving signals of her readiness. In other species, the traits that are successful in the selection process have mostly to do with genetic health and vitality. The human species has used its ability to construct cultural biases and mores that may override innate feminine preferences.

Over millennia, women in most societies have been forced (by such customs as arranged marriages and suppression of women in general) to accept the male traits that *men* prefer, creating a bias towards aggressiveness and 'success at any cost' behaviors whose deleterious effects can now be seen on a global scale. We are the victims of the mating choices of men and disempowered women.

**3.** Human male display has undergone a "runaway effect". Any male trait that is selected for by females becomes more pronounced through succeeding generations, because males will be born with that trait and females will be born with a preference for it. In a runaway effect, the trait will become so pronounced that it presents a danger to the male and, by extension, to the entire species. The classic example is the peacock's tail, which has evolved to be hazardous to the male bird's ability to escape predators. In this case, the runaway trait of the cumbersome tail is restrained by predation on the slowest males.

Many human males display by being loud, reckless and dangerous. So we see everything from unmuffled motorcycles through acts of violence to pursuit of status, even if such pursuits involve ecological destruction or war. When men indulge in such displays and are then chosen as mates, their predilections for dangerous and destructive displays will likely be passed on to the next generation's males.

**4.** Females of other species tend not to choose mates with traits that will endanger genetic survival. Since humans are at the top of the predator chain and the greatest dangers to our species are ourselves and our actions, men's runaway traits of aggression and destruction are now endangering our species and all others. Yet in a male-dominator society, those tend to be the behaviors that are rewarded. They are encouraged to intensify by making women believe that these are desirable traits to be passed down to their sons.

Our thesis is that it is up to women to recognize these runaway traits and refuse to choose men who display them, instead choosing men with traits that will work for sustaining the species and the world. Those traits may be hidden behind the false bravado that many men affect for survival, and only women can bring them to the fore. And while such traits may not be currently recognized as desirable by men, once women start choosing men who display them they *will become* desirable traits. Within a relatively short time, the adaptable males of our species will tend to show a preference for those traits and more men will display them openly and proudly.

We call men with the traits that will sustain our planet and its species, and who consider the effects of their actions, the ***Mindful Males***. When the Mindful Male traits become a desirable display, the snowball effect of sexual selection can begin. It is possible that within a few generations the Mindful Male will be the norm, while the acquisitive, violent male will be an unpopular aberration that will find it hard to find a willing mate.

## ALPHAS, BETAS AND MASKS

To aid your understanding and to communicate the complexity of men and women, here are some simple definitions of energies. As with all classification techniques, these are broad generalizations, intended not to categorize individuals, but to give us all a foundation on which to build a common understanding and communication.

## The Male Mask

This is the culturally essential protective shell which, to some extent, all men form around themselves from an early age. It protects them from emotional and physical danger by restraining the feminine characteristics that all men possess, but which are deemed unmanly in society. Men usually drop the Male Mask only in the presence of someone they really trust, such as a beloved life partner or family member, or in later life, when display becomes less necessary and their 'mindfulness' is allowed more freedom.

## Alpha-Beta Soup

We have divided humanity into the Alpha and Beta energies in order to be able to differentiate between the people out there who **are** initiating easy contact with the opposite sex and those who aren't. Since it is the Alphas, male *and* female, of the world who have less trouble initiating with the partners of their choice (even if their partnerships may not last long), the relationship part of our book is written with the Betas in mind. Alpha and Beta may seem hierarchical categories, in which the Alpha is by definition 'better' than the Beta, but for humans that is not necessarily the case. As the corporate world has discovered with the help of a Harvard Business School study, so-called Alpha traits are often destructive to the structure of an organization that depends on the combined skills of everyone involved.

Since true Alphas are a very small minority, Betas are by far the most numerous and therefore the most 'normal' of people. Our society, urged on by the media, has become so accustomed to idolizing the Alpha traits that men tend to be disturbed by being called Beta. Yet the "Alpha Male Syndrome"[3] is recognized as a real problem in organizations. We prefer to think of it as the Alpha-Mask Male Syndrome (see below).

Alpha strengths used by the rare true Alphas (perhaps 5% of the population) are useful and progressive, and the Alphas' intense focus and charisma can achieve great things. Their only weakness may be that they are not natural team-players, so may not spend enough time thinking about those lower on the totem pole that are actually fulfilling the Alpha's desires. They lack 'rear-view mirrors'.

Since Alphas are in such an extreme minority, and since Alphas are so accustomed to being first, we'll start with the Beta definitions.

## Beta Female

The Beta Female has received little attention in our society, which has always held up the Alpha Female version of the moment as the epitome of womanhood. But, as you will read later on, the Beta woman, when in the presence of a man, **is** an Alpha Female to him. Especially if he's a Beta Male.

About 95% of all women in the world are Beta Females, so they are the norm, however much they may feel left out by the mass media and movies. They are the foundation of humanity and the driving force of commerce. Most advertisements are aimed at Beta women, because they are the ones that hold the purse-strings and are the consumers that every company wants to attract, even as they create images of women that are hard to find anywhere in the real world.

---

[3] Kate Ludeman and Eddie Erlandson, *The Alpha Male Syndrome*, 2006, www.worthethic.com . Ludeman and Erlandson go into the corporate world to teach Alphas how to co-operate with fellow workers and staff and to lead without being the typical tyrannical Alpha or Alpha-Mask leader of the past.

Beta women are also the drivers of human evolution, through the choices they make in their mates. It is Sexual Selection in the hands of Beta Females that provides the gene pool for our species, so Betas are of the highest importance to the world, especially now that humans have the power to influence our environment to the point of destruction.

But despite their importance to the species and the planet, women who are living alone while yearning in their hearts for a partnership are surely Betas, not Alphas. They are deterred from initiating contact with men by fear of rejection and by unwillingness to risk being labeled as too 'easy' or aggressive.

Beta women, having been blinded to their Feminine power, generally do not understand the extent to which they intimidate men. All men, Betas in particular, but also the Alphas, are in awe of the Feminine and its sexual promise, which is the greatest urge in every species, including ours.

We know that once the Feminine is understood and utilized by Beta women, everything is possible – lasting and fulfilling relationships, a more peaceful existence and partnership with men in every facet of our culture – since their sheer numbers could bring us to the tipping point of culture change.

## Beta Male

Being called a Beta Male is by no means the slur that our Alpha-worshipping media culture would have us believe it is. Indeed the media depend upon the Beta population to read and watch their productions. Almost all human beings *are* Betas and it is best to regard Beta-ness as the norm, with Alpha-ness as a rare occurrence. That's why Alphas stand out so much. Our guess is that if Alphas were in the majority, the human race would not have survived as long as it has.

There is therefore a whole spectrum of Beta behaviors. Beta men, each with their unique personal qualities, are not as driven or focused as Alphas, and lack the Alpha's charismatic traits. There are Betas who follow, but there are also Betas who are completely independent and in charge of their own lives but who are not comfortable in positions of absolute command. They may have confidence in their own abilities, find purpose and fulfillment in their lives, but may not wish to be in the limelight.

They may be in charge of a team in which collaboration is more evident than would be the case in Alpha leadership. They can lead by example of their acquired skills in their chosen field. They are more likely to form consensus-building groups and alliances, looking for the support of a community, rather than being the classic Lone Wolf Alphas and Alpha-Masks, who will strive for 'success' at any cost to those around them. That's not to say that there aren't Lone Wolf Betas, but they are more likely to be separating themselves from society as recluses than trying to run it.

Beta men and women are the foundation of human society, doing all the work that needs doing and not usually seeking the limelight. They may have fame thrust upon them, if they do something out of the ordinary, such as writing some revolutionary software or composing a great song. But mostly, they live their lives among their peers, without being the centers of attention and without wanting to be.

Unfortunately, those men living alone yet wishing to be in partnership are most likely Betas. Alphas can call their own shots without thinking, but Betas in general are far more circumspect of exposing themselves to rejection. This book was written to help these men and the women with whom they could be partnered. Our hope is that, with the help of their female partners, Beta Males can become **Mindful Men**, the kind of men who are comfortable in partnership with women and in expressing their feminine intelligence alongside their masculine focus.

Also, the Alpha-Mask Males (see below) come from the pool of Betas, those who want to conform to society's fantasy of Alpha behavior, perhaps from being influenced by movies, or by having to be aggressive, even violent, in order to survive in their environment.

## Alpha Male

This man is born with basic traits of self-assurance and charisma, physical strength, intelligence, emotional control, independence, competitiveness, attractive or imposing physical appearance, courage, total focus on goals and a need to lead. The hallmark of the true Alpha is that they inspire respect for their vision, courage and focus without having to coerce others into becoming disciples.

The true Alpha Male is not driven by insecurity and fear and has no need for violence or over-aggressive tactics to achieve his goals. Alphas have historically been held as the epitome of manhood by other men, and while the world needs the true Alpha qualities of courage and independent thinking, they must sometimes be tempered with foresight of the consequences of his actions, something that Alphas often lack or show no concern for. Their competitiveness with their peers can create friction and create disharmony among their followers and employees.

This has been recognized as a liability in corporate management, where the old paradigm of the all-powerful boss is slowly being replaced. However, the Alpha Male has lost none of his attractiveness in politics, and the military is still built around blind obedience to the Alpha figurehead. Unfortunately, those two institutions are inextricably linked in countries like the USA, in which the go-for-broke Alpha is still worshipped as the paradigm of the All-American male. **Only the influence of the Feminine will be able to divert *unmindful* Alpha Males into using their great abilities for the good of all.**

The Mindful Alpha Male and Alpha Female have the greatest potential for positive leadership by example. The Alpha Males are the focused leaders who, if we can get their attention and help them to co-create rather than charge ahead alone, may help lead us all into positive cultural change.

## Alpha-Mask Male – the Dangerous Wanna-be

Alpha-Mask Males are Betas hidden behind an exaggerated Male Mask. These are the men who have been, for example, so injured by rejection or abuse that they have constructed an elaborate shield that allows them to show indifference in times of fear. The more extreme Alpha-Mask Males are 'over the top' in their masculine traits – super macho, emotionally stunted, possibly violent, intent on their survival at any cost. Their drive, which may have been drilled into them by family, peers and mentors, is in craving respect, no matter how it is achieved.

Most often, unfortunately, the Alpha-Mask Male has been responsible for some of the most destructive human acts and is often mistaken for true Alphas by Betas. Their kind of overaggressive leadership and willingness to ride roughshod over others has long been held up as the standard of leadership in popular culture, so much so that those who emulate them can find their way to the highest levels of business, politics and the military.

In such cases, the 'respect' that the Alpha-Mask craves and thinks he is receiving may only be fawning sycophancy from followers and copycats seeking their own aggrandizement. We see it all too often in political 'strongmen', dictators and despotic corporate CEOs. They do not take No for an answer, they rule with an iron fist and the bloody history of humanity is full of such men. Leading by instilling fear in their followers and destroying their opponents has been the hallmark of the most repressive societies. Political polarization without compromise is a typical Alpha-Mask tactic, which makes a mockery of public discourse and democracy.

Whatever the initial impetus for a man to become an Alpha-Mask Male, they are a pervasive influence on our media-driven, sound-bite society. The image of the Alpha-Mask as the strong, win-at-all-costs superman is an easy one to assimilate, and is attractive to adolescents looking for their own identity. It is unfortunate that more of these future Alpha-Mask Males are not guided towards less destructive behavior.

The influence of patriarchal values has been so pervasive for so long, that our norms are slow to change, and our dominator cultures love the Alpha-Mask Male. He is useful as cannon fodder in the endless string of wars that he is taught to anticipate with glee. He is the aggressive, violent member of the herd who thinks he is *Somebody*, and who can be brainwashed into any action his superiors demand of him. He is the gang member who continues to give patriarchy the ammunition it needs to keep his people down by his violent acts and his prison record. He is the avid consumer of every product that he thinks will prove he is *A Real Man*, from straight-pipe Harleys to weapons for recreational slaughter. We have seen Alpha-Mask Males as Presidents of the United States and as fanatical terrorists.

Yet all this behavior is founded, however unconsciously, on the male need to display, to be noticed, which gives a woman the power to 'civilize' the Alpha-Mask Male. If a woman can win over one of these men and get past the over-aggressive exterior, she may find a frightened boy, whose sensitivities are raw; someone with great depths of feeling just waiting for the gentle touch to bring them out from behind the Mask.

## Alpha Female

**Any woman becomes an Alpha when she is in the company of a man.** Men feel it instinctively, and just by being herself, she naturally assumes the Alpha role between them, thanks to the biological power of the Feminine.

Then there are those rare women who are true born Alphas who display some or all of the following: intelligence, charismatic self-assurance, emotional strength, attractive or imposing physical appearance, skill in forming alliances and building community, deep listening.

The true Alpha Female has already redefined seduction to her own ends, appealing to the better side in all of us, making no secret of her vulnerability to male force, and thereby winning the protection of men in a male-dominated arena. She does not lose sight of her nurturing side, because that is what she uses to gain allies. She is not ashamed of the effects of her sensual nature on men and is not afraid to use them to good effect around those who oppose her.

She has the holistic vision that is the specialty of the female brain, seeing fully the consequences of her actions and understanding the strength that comes from teamwork and partnership in all areas. Her charisma and charm help her to attract women and men in willing cooperation, making coercion and overly aggressive tactics unnecessary in achieving her goals. Alpha Women leaders create inclusive and horizontal cultures rather than pyramid-shaped hierarchies with themselves perched precariously at the top.

### Alpha-Mask Female – playing a man's game

These women are determined to win by any means and will adopt the qualities of the Male Mask to hide their true feminine selves. Alpha-Mask women use male tactics to gain power in male-dominated pursuits, often forsaking feminine power for abusive and coercive force.

When we talk about women as nurturers and seducers, we often hear reference made to powerful women who are perceived as Alphas in our society. The woman often cited as an example of the Alpha Female is Margaret Thatcher. But we regard her as the quintessential *Alpha-Mask* Female, opposed to consensus, belittling and coercive. Instead of creating partnerships and alliances, she alienated and polarized both those who supported her and her opposition; the antithesis of the alliance-making Feminine. Her success-at-any-cost campaign was in the male preserve of government, in which she made her controversial mark by assuming male strategies, holding sway over a Cabinet of Ministers that included no women.

To call her a true Alpha Female denigrates Alphas, and skews the public's vision of the Feminine. Men understand the Thatcher approach, as it is similar to the male hierarchy-building tactic. It makes her easier for men to understand and to oppose, and she appealed to the boarding-school-educated Conservative politicians of her era, perhaps because she reminded them of the stern matrons about whom they had secret erotic fantasies. Just as 'seduction' has been given negative connotations in a male-dominator society, so has 'Alpha Female'. The true Alpha woman is a powerful evolutionary co-creator, not a despotic governess.

## Alpha Effects

So what does that all mean in our day-to-day existence? Who is to blame for the state of affairs the human race finds itself struggling with? Unless you believe in some god or other being the micro-manager of everyone's lives, there's nobody to blame but the collective cultural influence and our own genetic tampering. By trying to "fix" the human genome through selective breeding that has gone off course, we have diverted the course of our natural evolution.

We're not talking about mad scientists here, but the choices of mates that have been made through the centuries, influenced first by patriarchy in general and then by patriarchal dilution of trust in the female power of selection. So we have a preponderance of Alpha and Alpha-Mask behavior leading the species, which is, due to the belief systems that their cliques have created over millennia, anti-Nature and thus anti-human.

In *Evolution for Everyone*, by Professor David Sloan Wilson[4] is an illustration of men's tampering with Nature to make it 'better', and also of the effects of Alpha behavior when selected for over generations. Wilson tells of a genetic experiment carried out by a poultry scientist who wanted to test ways of increasing egg production in chickens through selective breeding.

The hens were caged in groups of nine, and in the first experiment, he selected the most productive individual hens from several different cages to breed a new generation of Alphas, which would then be housed together in groups of nine from which the most productive individuals would be selected, and so on.

In the second experiment, he selected entire groups of nine hens from the most productive cages. He kept the groups together as groups and bred them to create more groups, from which the most productive groups would be selected.

Six generations later, the most productive individual hens that were removed from their groups had produced a generation of psychopaths. There were only three surviving hens in the cage, the other six having been pecked to death, and the survivors were almost featherless from constant attacks on each other. Egg production had plummeted, even though, in each generation, the most productive hens had been selected for breeding. It seems that the original single hens had increased their egg production by suppressing the productivity of their cage-mates, and those traits were passed down through each generation as the most productive/aggressive ones were selected for breeding.

---

[4] *Evolution for Everyone: How Darwin's Theory Can Change the Way We Think About Our Lives*, 2007. A wonderful book on evolution, which we happened across in an airport bookstore. Synchronicity once again, and a great read while traveling.

## Seduction Redefined

The second groups of hens gave rise to cages full of plump, well-feathered "happy" hens, whose egg production had increased dramatically. The hens that lived as a micro-society to produce lots of eggs were healthy and lived harmoniously, having been selected for their co-operative traits.

We could categorize the top-laying single hens as Alphas, who became the 'best' by beating all the others and competing with them, using violence if necessary, to 'win'. When too many Alphas were trying to beat each other, the whole system collapsed as they fought each other for top honors and ended up killing themselves. Sound familiar?

We could also categorize the second groups of hens as the Betas, the ones whose co-operative, productive, community-oriented traits were selected for and created a healthy society.

The whole experiment illustrates something about humans too. The desire to always be tinkering and 'improving' Nature's systems is in itself the kind of behavior that has edged us toward our destruction, especially when it is carried out at the expense of other living beings. When this is systematized by corporations and the governments they influence, without accountability for their actions, it gives free rein to Alphas and Alpha-Masks to indulge in their most aggressive and antisocial behavior.

Perhaps it's time for the Beta Revolution, where the Beta is the new Alpha, where co-operation is more important than making it to the 'top' and the Precautionary Principle is valued more than 'success' at any price. Perhaps we can no longer endure the Alpha-Mask behavior that endangers us all, and we must begin to make the Mindful Man and true partnership between the sexes the essential paradigm.

There's evidence that this idea is creeping into mainstream consciousness, with nice Beta guys acing out the Alpha-Masks as the romantic heroes. Kindness and mindfulness is sexy![5]

## The Functional Feminine and Functional Masculine

We've already mentioned the Functional Feminine and Masculine, and we think their definitions are fairly intuitively understood, but just in case you're confused, here are some qualities of each of them.

**The Functional Feminine** represents all those traits that give women their innate biological power, and which inspired historical worship of the feminine principle. Women can give birth to new life, the future of their species. Women hold the power to alter the path of evolution through their selection of mates and their influence over their mates and offspring.

The Functional Feminine holds the ability to see the Big Picture. While men focus, women multi-task, while men obsess over details and facts, women consider side effects and use intuition and empathy. The Functional Feminine knows how to nurture, protect and provide for the 'nest', whether that be home or the greater community. It is emotional, visceral humanity, offering comfort, pleasure and warmth. It is the *sensible* in every way – the taking in of holistic information through the senses, using common sense, intuition and sensitivity to emotional and physical needs to create solutions. When given free rein, the Functional Feminine is the guardian of the planet, in tune with the rhythms of Nature. It is powerful vulnerability and tender resilience.

The awe in which the female form and women in general are held is evidence of the sensual power of the Functional Feminine. Men are enthralled by women, which can be frightening for men who feel

---

[5] Kimberly Dawn Neumann, *The New Hollywood Heartthrob: The Nice Guy*, Lemondrop.com, October 31, 2008.

## Seduction Redefined

diminished by their unfulfilled desires. The saying "The egg knows more than the sperm" is a colloquial simplification of the fact that the human egg is very selective in allowing a single sperm to be engulfed by it and fuse to it.

Far from being the passive receptor of the first, strongest, fastest-swimming sperm, the outer layer of the egg, the zona pellucida, acts as an adaptability test of the sperm. Proteins in the membrane act as docking ports for the chosen sperm, but they are constantly changing their 'entry codes', so the sperm must keep up with them to 'crack the code' and gain entry. Sperm want to get the job over and done with as soon as they can, while the egg wants to slow the process down in the interests of quality![6]

The choosiness of the egg may be intuitively understood by men, perceived as a threat to the male urge to procreate as much as possible and partly responsible for the restrictions of women's freedom and influence that have survived to the present day. Even if the actual process has not been understood until recently, the power of a woman to reject a man's advances definitely was, hence the introduction of arranged marriages, women as chattel or bargaining chips in the male struggle for status.

When women use force rather than their inherent power, or when they are cowed into submission and denial of their own power, the **Dysfunctional** Feminine arises. It feeds, imitates and celebrates the Dysfunctional Masculine. It has helped to erode women's liberties, drive men's greed, support war and pervert the evolution of our species.

---

[6] Swanson and Vacquier, *The Rapid Evolution of Reproductive Proteins*, Nature Feb 2002, vol. 3; Natalie Angier, *New Rules in Sperm and Egg's Cat-and-Mouse Game*, New York Times, Feb 27, 2001

**The Functional Masculine** is the power that men have to work for the common good of the species as the complement to the Feminine. Every great thing created by men is created, fundamentally, for the attention of women, and the Functional Masculine feels no threat in adjusting to the desires of women. When women are allowed to choose their mates (and when they use the Functional Feminine to do so), they choose kindness, generosity, humor, intelligence, altruism, curiosity and a host of non-destructive traits in their mates. These are all parts of the Functional Masculine, which also embodies controlled assertiveness, mental focus, adaptability, inventiveness and other survival traits selected by our distant foremothers and thereby inherited from our forefathers.

The Functional Masculine is not threatened by the Functional Feminine, but understands instinctively the complementary powers of each to advance civilization. When the Masculine resists adaptation to the needs of the Feminine and the species, it stresses physical force over intelligence, violence over channeled aggression, and creates the **Dysfunctional** Masculine.

The Dysfunctional Masculine has brought our species to the brink of destruction by disregarding the deep-rooted and essential connection of the Functional Feminine to the Earth and its preservation and to the Functional Masculine and its adaptability. The Dysfunctional Masculine has fought the Feminine at every turn, seeing only a threat to its fragile, distorted self-image of masculinity. When the Dysfunctional Masculine feels rejected or threatened by women, its reaction is likely to be overly aggressive as a display of its 'strength'.

There is nothing strong in the Dysfunctional Masculine, except the desire to display superiority in any way possible, regardless of consequences. It is the non-adaptive, immature, bully face of a doomed breed, and we have been deep in its grip for thousands of years. Its diversion of evolution has finally come home to roost and our species **must** adapt now.

The Functional Feminine can turn the Dysfunctional Masculine around and we must create the partnership between the Functional Feminine and Masculine, or we will suffer the fate of every other species that the Dysfunctional Masculine, with support from the Dysfunctional Feminine, has caused to become extinct.

## *Eros* and *Agape*

There are two kinds of love that happen to everyone in a relationship that progresses from sexual attraction to partnership, from *eros* to *agape*. We received this explanation from a friend many years ago. We don't know who wrote it, but it still rings true.

### *Eros*

This love is an all-consuming, desperate yearning for the beloved, who is perceived as different, mysterious and elusive. The depth of love is measured by the intensity of obsession with the loved one. There is little time or attention for other interests or pursuits because so much energy is focused on recalling past encounters or imaginary future ones. Often, great obstacles must be overcome and thus there is an element of suffering in true love. Another indication of the depth of love is the willingness to endure pain and hardship for the sake of the relationship. Associated with this love are feelings of excitement, rapture, drama, anxiety, tension, mystery and yearning.

### *Agape*

This love is a partnership to which two caring people are deeply committed. These people share many basic values, interests and goals. The depth of love is measured by the mutual trust and respect they feel toward each other. Their relationship allows each to be more fully expressive, creative and productive in the world. There is much joy in shared experiences both past and present, as well as those that are anticipated. Each views the other as his/her dearest and most cherished friend. Another measure of the depth of love is willingness to look honestly at oneself in order to promote growth of the relationship and deepening of intimacy. Associated with this love are feelings of serenity, security, devotion, understanding, companionship, mutual support and comfort.

## Now it begins

Now you have the vocabulary down, please enjoy the rest of the book as we tell you our story, the revelations it has brought and our dreams for the future.

# CHAPTER ONE

## Donna: Seduction

### *Stepping into Power as the Feminine Seductress*

*Cleopatra was physically unexceptional and had no political power, yet both Caesar and Antony, brave and clever men, saw none of this. What they saw was a woman who constantly transformed herself before their eyes, a one-woman spectacle.*
Robert Greene, *The Art of Seduction*

## Donna's Redefining Moment

I had met and talked with Paul at several public events, but that evening he was sitting on a chair in front of an open fire after a community potluck party at my house — his face golden and smiling. The last remaining couple and Paul and I were talking, and I surprised even myself when I placed my hands on his knees and asked, "Paul, may I kiss you?" He smiled, so I leaned over and kissed him.

The other couple graciously and quickly left and then we kissed again and again and again. He slid off his chair to the floor with me.

As we slipped down, intuitively I whispered in his ear, "No strings attached!" Those magic words of freedom launched all the collective spontaneity that you've ever seen in movies — ahhh, passion incarnate.

There was a moment of post-passion giggle when I asked him how old he was (I didn't have my glasses on!). When he answered "Forty-two" I realized "Oh my god, I'm twenty-one years older than you!" It was quite unnerving and I had had no intention of 'taking advantage' of a younger man.

He left soon after our brains re-engaged. Next morning, I awoke with a start, knowing my body was not the same body as 24 hours before! Newly sprouting buds of desire slowly began to open and by 5 p.m. I was in full blossom. By nightfall, I could imagine the moonlight falling passionately on my intimate stranger, Paul. God was squeezing me in the dark. God would not stop.

All I knew was that I wanted more, more and more. Why now and why Paul? A swirl of questions, contradictions and self-doubts engulfed me. "When will I see him again? When? When? When? Tonight? Will he call? Can I wait? Must I wait for The Call as I have done most of my life, trying to remain patient and demure? I kissed him, he didn't kiss me. Was the sex good enough for him to want to see me again? What about the age difference? *How long must I wait until he calls?*"

And then I reached a point where I let my instincts take over. I answered my doubts with different questions, "I've chosen him, so why wait at all for his call?" and "What do I have to lose if I call him?" Then, after the internal argument ended, I said, "I have nothing invested yet, so why not be assertive and make the call? I'm tired of waiting for the Alpha Male/Knight in Shining Armor to seduce me; I shall seduce this man!"

This time around, instead of caring about "forever", I adopted the "no strings attached", pleasure approach. It was purely intuitive, little did I know it, but this method proved to be essential for keeping Paul within range of my seductive strength. It was all about staying in the "NOW."

Passion! One day at a time. No strings attached. *Full speed ahead.*

## Re-emerging Intuition

Can you see yourself doing something like this? Believe me, I would never have thought myself capable of such forwardness if I hadn't had faith in my intuition about Paul. But once the initiating was done, I realized how natural it all seemed. There was something about this man that told me he was right for me, and when that happens we have only ourselves to blame if we don't act on it.

If you are one of the millions of women desiring a long-term committed relationship, it is up to you to be the sensual woman you were meant to be, to follow your intuition and take action when you find a man with the traits you most desire. Your courage is needed in a time when the single-person household is the fastest-growing segment of housing arrangements in the U.S., and men and women are more isolated, doubtful and misinformed about one another than ever before. *Seduction Redefined* will change your life and you will be part of a new beginning for loving partnership on the planet!

I reflect upon my previous marriages and realize that my husbands were men who had chosen me, and it was I that had left them, looking for – what? The relationship with my third husband, for example, ended not through any fault of his, but because I needed the creative collaboration I felt was lacking, once our joint projects of many years together were finished and we each retreated to our separate work. I sought a person with writing skills and political and intellectual pursuits to complement my activist skills. At the time I didn't yet know that I had intuited them in Paul.

Looking back after all the years of living in partnership with Paul, I can trace how I followed my intuitive choice of him as a partner and became a living testament to what Charles Darwin called Sexual Selection, females selecting males as mates, rather than the males doing the choosing. Alongside Natural Selection of survival traits and competition by males for the attention of females, Sexual Selection is a major driving force in evolution. The selection by females of certain characteristics in males creates the propensity for those characteristics to continue and become more pronounced in males and also increases the desire for those characteristics in female offspring.

In humans, this process has been ongoing from the dawn of the species, but in our times women are heavily influenced by the current definition of "modern civilization" which is Alpha-male oriented. Being raised in a culture with this skew, I was told to wait on the sidelines for "the call" and to suppress my own female sexual needs, intuition and power. But the BIG new thing for me was that my undying curiosity of why it felt so right to pursue Paul and break down his defenses led me to begin my research into seduction, which later led to peace activism and empowerment of women. He didn't know at first that I was right for him, but I did, and that was enough to begin a serious seduction. And, as we later discovered in our research, the egg knows more than the sperm, meaning the egg actively chooses which sperm will be allowed to fertilize her.

Recent research shows that a woman's reproductive system is choosy and wants sperm to display their suitability.[7] Gynecologists used to believe that if a couple couldn't get pregnant and the man's semen was "normal", then the problem was the woman. It turns out

---

[7] Sarah Robertson, Immune regulation of conception and embryo implantation – all about quality control? Journal of Reproductive Immunology, vol. 85: 51-57, 2009

it may just be that if the display by the sperm is inadequate to convince the egg, it will not be accepted.

## Intuition or *Eros*?

I have been asked how I knew that I was acting from my intuition and not just from my erotic drive and sexual attraction to Paul. How can a woman tell if she's just ready for a fling or has found the man that is best suited to her as a true partner? I answer that you can never be one hundred percent sure that you're not just acting on your libidinous impulses, but if later you feel the need to see him again, and it feels right just being with him, even without the sex, that's a good sign. If you stay in the Now and don't weave any fantasies of long-term relationship, if you pay attention to how you feel when he's with you and it feels better than when he isn't, that's another good sign. And if, as the relationship progresses, it becomes clear to you that you and he are a good match – for Now – that's enough of a sign to keep the seduction going.

It all depends on the balance of pleasure versus pain. If you're going to expend your energy to seduce this man, uncertainty of the outcome or of your motives is perfectly fine in the Now, but unease or discomfort in his presence is not. That would be your intuition telling you that something is not right.

The effects of carrying on a seduction will give you confidence in your Feminine and in overcoming any uncertainty of yourself. It will also increase your intuition and attune you to the warning signs in his behavior that may signal the time for you to stop seducing and move on.

Remember – *The egg knows more than the sperm.*

## The Ultimate Feminine Power

When you hear the word seduction, you might think of exotic *femmes fatales*, weaving spells of spice and forbidden sex – or dashing and depraved men leading innocent women astray. The word "seducer" conjures thoughts of legendary individuals of great power taking advantage of everyday people.

> **Outdated Myths and Mores**
>
> Men have to make the first move in courtship
>
> Women who take the lead are desperate, aggressive or just sluts
>
> Men do not fear women
>
> Only "beautiful" Alpha women can choose their partners
>
> **Redefined Seduction Truths**
>
> Women, not men, should make the first move in courtship
>
> Women's initiative in courtship is not only natural but also essential to the survival of the species
>
> Men are in awe of women and will adapt to their desires
>
> Every woman possesses the power to select and seduce her chosen mate.

Until now, modern women have been reluctant to be thought of as seducers because of the word's historical connection to depravity and an overwhelming passion, followed by rejection and disgrace. The stigma surrounding the word seduction comes from centuries of social and sexual repression of women[8] reinforced by patriarchy, religion and movie fantasy. This has given rise to myths and mores that are now outdated.

## How Did We Get Here?

Out of the myths of the past has evolved into the Hollywood image of woman as the passive recipient of man's romantic skills, taking no part in the seduction other than swooning in his manly arms. Any woman of free will knows in her heart that this is a failing archetype. Yet and still, if a woman is attracted to a man she meets,

---

[8] Deborah Rhode, *Speaking of Sex: The Denial of Gender Inequality*: Rhode's book, published in 1997, refutes the generally held belief that gender inequality is a thing of the past.

it is the norm for her to wait for her phone to ring or email to beckon – signaling that she has received The Call.[9]

Not until my late thirties, did I realize that I could be "assertive," but unfortunately always with a coating of sarcasm. Sarcasm was and is to this day a mechanism (very popular in San Francisco) to protect vulnerability, keeping fragile feelings locked inside. My "tough" outer shield only served to push away aggressive Alpha-oriented males or to terrify the kind of Mindful Male who craved partnership, not warfare, with a woman.

I know what happened in my life due to ignorance, body shame and belief in the myths. I've seen the damage caused in other women and men's lives by their fear, lack of knowledge and hopelessness. Here's why I place blame on culture and religion – my first husband, the first Alpha Male to choose me, when he was still my fiancé, took me to bed and I became pregnant. He told me that, being a good Catholic, he could not introduce me to his mother if I were pregnant, because that would mean we had had sex before marriage, so he took me to an illegal abortionist, who damaged my uterus, preventing my having future children. I married him in a Catholic church, hemorrhaging beneath my white wedding dress.

You may say that things have changed in this new century, because there are so many more assertive women. People say to us all the time that they feel that women are choosing their partners. Yes, the Alpha women are choosing, but they're in the minority. Our studies indicate that the majority of women are still uncomfortable with owning their Feminine Power, they are still waiting for The

---

[9] Ellen Fein and Sherrie Schneider, *The Rules*: The book that tells women they have to play hard to get, never call a man, hold out for the expensive gifts and generally prolong the myth that women can beat up on men emotionally and expect to get away with it. The bible for those who wish to widen the gender gap and prolong the misery of single men and women.

Call that will validate that they are worthy of being "chased." I want women to know that their worth is in their wisdom to select a good potential partner and to initiate a relationship using their innate powers of feminine seduction. Their worth is in our ability to move their partners into a mindful, loving partnership.

As a matchmaker, I have found over and over that after I have informed both the man and the woman about each other, I advise the woman to call the man and she will say, "Oh no, I couldn't! He MUST call me!" And usually nothing comes of it. Aaaargh!! Well, I say wake up, Sleeping Beauty, and join us on a journey to learn about your true feminine power.

About ninety per cent of the male population would be overjoyed to receive your implicit approval of them by your initiating a seduction, in so doing reducing their fear of rejection and increasing your own self-esteem. So go ahead and create a loving partnership with a fully Functional Masculine Male by owning your power as a wise, passionate woman who can redefine seduction as a force for love and peace in the world.

## The Basics of Feminine Power

*[Seductresses] defuse [men's] fear by balancing intimacy and TLC with non-maternal sizzle. The backdrag to mother and her maternal sweets is inherent in eros, a powerful, primordial pull. Yet it coexists with female autonomy and sex appeal and may even depend upon them for peak efficiency.* Betsy Prioleau[10]

---

[10] *Seductress: Women Who Ravished the World and Their Lost Art of Love*. An impassioned study of the great seductresses in all their forms. Prioleau argues for a return to the unabashedly sensual woman in our Barbie-doll society.

In Nature, an Alpha is the most powerful animal in a group. From the point of view of men, consciously or unconsciously, every woman is an Alpha. She's a strong being with power over them. Perhaps you don't feel like an Alpha, but if you tap into your intuitive as I did while seducing Paul, you will know that every woman that cares to use it has Alpha power over men. It's biological, it's genetic, it's instinctual, it's hard-wired into every woman, and the reactions to it are hard-wired into every man. It's the power of Darwin's Sexual Selection, a biological mechanism so important to life that it is a driving force behind evolution itself. And its power is in your hands!

*If the female of most other species initiates partnership, why not the female of the human species?*

## The Nature of Nurture

Some of the Feminine's power derives from the fertility cycle that governs women's emotional and physical lives. Women are affected by the same rhythms as the Earth itself and are constantly reminded of the elemental nature of our bodies. We get a sense of our life-giving place in the natural world and a connection to the forces of Nature around us. It is a grand perspective of our bodies that helps us feel the interconnectedness of everything around and inside us. It is the rhythm of life.

As we enter the life-giving cycle of ovulation and menstruation, we learn to experience our nurturing power. It expresses itself in every interaction we have; with friends, partners, family and children; with community, at parties and celebrations; with pets, gardens and nature; in cooking and our own health; in building a home for our loved ones and ourselves. It is the emotional connection with the rest of the world that comes naturally to women and from which most men insulate themselves. Most women have no idea how detached and fearful men are, comparatively speaking. That simple difference affects every perception. Both men and women understand intuitively that the Feminine is the place to find compassion, comfort and respite from the cruel world.

When you want to soothe a man into being comfortable with your company, you simply do what comes naturally; be a woman. When you approach a man and start talking to him in a natural way, he is bound to react positively at first. He will feel flattered and pleased that you would come over to him. It's a compliment to him to give him your attention.

I am six feet tall but I still have the advantage of being seen by most men as the weaker sex, therefore vulnerable and worthy of protection. Size, shape, weight or height are all the same to the male. Certainly, he has built-in preferences for young, healthy women, signaled by certain body characteristics,[11] but any woman's attention will start unconscious physical reactions.

A man's chivalrous inclination makes him naturally attentive to you and open to suggestion, even while he's mentally undressing you and he is entering the first stages of sexual arousal. It's natural for him to be doing this; he may not even be aware of his mental and physical processes, the impulse may never even enter his consciousness, but whenever a heterosexual man is around a woman he hasn't met before, his body is beginning to prepare itself for sex. Doesn't matter if he's a "saint" or a "sinner," the biological processes are in motion.

Research shows that women's hormonal cycles influence men's attraction to them without either of them necessarily knowing it. It has been found that when female strippers are in the maximally

---

[11] Standards of beauty - visual, vocal and chemical cues that reveal healthy characteristics - differ between cultures and generations, but the underlying 'rules' of forming beauty ideals have cross-cultural universality. Grammer, Fink, Møller, Thornhill: *Darwinian aesthetics: sexual selection and the biology of beauty*; (2003) Biological Reviews.

fertile part of their cycle, male customers tip them more.¹² And when in the fertile phase, women are more concerned with looking beautiful and buying cosmetics than when they're in the non-fertile phase, when it's more about good food than looking good!

So just being friendly to a man makes him sexually aroused to some extent. It's an evolutionary adaptation to minimize the chance of missing a "reproductive opportunity"¹³. If that alarms you, be aware that most men won't act on their arousal, because it's only a minor titillation and so frequent, what with every waitress and check-out woman smiling and wishing him a nice day, that he couldn't act on them all even if he wanted to or actually felt it.

Don't think badly of him, use it to your advantage. Be aware that if you find a man even remotely attractive, your body is making its own automatic preparations for sex, too. It's all about our species' need for procreation (just like every other species on the planet) and pleasure, because *in every human body there are two neural pathways to pleasure – sex and food!*

> *Woman is the Creator of the universe*
> *She is the very body of the universe;*
> *Woman is the support of the three worlds,*
> *She is the very essence of our body.*
> *There is no other happiness as*
> *that which woman can procure.*
> *There is no other way than*
> *that which woman can open to us.*
> *Never has there been, is there,*
> *will there be*
> *A fortune the like of woman, no kingdom,*
> *No place of pilgrimage, yoga, prayer,*
> *Mystic formula, asceticism, wealth.*
>
> Shaktisangama-Tantra II.52

---

[12] Gad Saad, *The Consuming Instinct: What Juicy Burgers, Ferraris, Pornography and Gift-Giving Reveal About Human Nature.* Prometheus Books, 2011

[13] Haselton, Martie G. & Buss, David M., *Error Management Theory: a new perspective on biases in cross-sex mind reading*; Journal of Personality and Social Psychology, January 2000, vol. 78, no. 1, 81-91. How men and women misread each other and the evolutionary reasons for it.

## The Power of the Vulnerable

In many traditional societies, before the western conquerors and missionaries got to them, women were the arbiters of justice, the umpires of combat, the glue that held community together. While the men may have been fierce warriors, the women had the Feminine, which was, as it still is, a force for social stability, peace and civilization.

In the Eastern Mediterranean were found the remnants of a peaceful society of partnership between men and women, in which the Feminine was revered and there was no need to build fortified cities.[14]

In Australia, when two men wanted to fight over something, the women would stand by and let them blow off some steam, then step in and stop the fight before the men killed each other.[15]

More recently, in Nigeria, women entered an oil-drilling installation and simply *threatened* to remove their clothes to shame the men of ChevronTexaco into providing simple necessities for the villages in the area, and succeeded.[16]

In Liberia, which has suffered through two civil wars since its founding, women finally had had enough of the brutality and bloodshed, and gathered peacefully in public every day to confront

---

[14] Riane Eisler, *The Chalice and the Blade: Our History, Our Future*, 1988. The classic book on partnership societies of the past, building on the work by Maria Gimbutas, who turned archeology upside down by, for the first time, giving a more rounded interpretation of findings than the predominantly male discipline ever had.

[15] Robert Lawlor, *Voices of the First Day*, 1991. A study of Australian aborigines and their culture and Dreamtime beliefs.

[16] Ruth Rosen, *The Power of Peaceful Protest*, SF Chronicle, July 15, 2002. This was the inspiration for Donna's peace organization, BaringWitness.org

the armed thugs and call for the killing to stop.[17] Because of their bravery, the worst of the violence ceased and a woman was elected President.

In Colombia, women have taken to becoming latter-day Lysistratas by refusing sex to the men in their lives until the women's needs are met. In one instance, the wives and girlfriends of gang members withheld sex from their partners during a violent period in which 480 people were killed. Within ten days, the men conceded and turned their weapons in to the authorities. In another town, three hundred women refused sex to their husbands until the men pressured local authorities to repair the only road to the outside world and the nearest hospital.[18]

Juchitán, in the Mexican state of Oaxaca, is famous for what is termed a matriarchy, but that term implies that matriarchies are like patriarchal hierarchies, only with women at the top of the pyramid. What are called matriarchies by male historians and sociologists are really partnership societies. When women and men use their complementary skills in harmony, there is distribution of labor and no need for the power struggles of a hierarchy. Partnership societies are 'horizontal' societies, rather than 'vertical'.

That is wonderfully apparent in Juchitán, where the men are farmers and provide food for the table and for market. The women take the produce to market and do all the business, and are in charge of the money. The men and women are happy with the arrangement. The money is not all spent on booze, the women are full of self-esteem and sexual 'juice', so the men are happy, well fed and hard working. The communities are close-knit and what stands

---

[17] Abigail Disney & Gini Reticker, *Pray the Devil Back to Hell*, documentary film, 2008, in *The Huffington Post*, July 17, 2008, Melissa Silverstein.

[18] The protest has been dubbed the Crossed Legs Strike. http://www.globalpost.com/print/5661102

## Seduction Redefined

out is that the towns look freshly scrubbed, unlike so much of rural Mexico, and form the perfect backdrop for the women in their brightly colored, embroidered dresses. [19]

The only apparent downside is that the macho males of Mexico look down on Juchitán's men as wimps, and the tabloid press runs stories accusing the women of rampant promiscuity. But the men just smile, knowing they are in partnership with the sexiest women in the country, and the women dismiss the slanders as sour grapes, and get back to business.

While there will always be men (and some women) who will seek to suppress the power of the Feminine through ridicule, violence and macho-posturing displays of physical force, it is only because they are intimidated by the power of women to civilize, to alter men's behavior, to teach them when to give up the childish aggressive displays they wish to prolong, to show them how to live in family, in community, in the world. The awesome power of the Feminine[20] is within you, it simply needs to be recognized and given free rein.

---

[19] *Blossoms of Fire*, directed by Maureen Gosling and Ellen Osborne, is a beautifully-made documentary on the Zapotecan women of Juchitán de Zaragoza. 2000.

[20] André van Lysebeth, Tantra: The Cult of the Feminine.

# CHAPTER TWO

## Paul: Seduction

### *Receiving the Gift of Feminine Seduction*

*As men and women we collude to stage an elaborate costume masquerade in which we chat casually or dance closely cheek to cheek, but are not at all who we seem to be. Our choreographies are so convincing, even to ourselves, that we get taken by our own performances and see ourselves as who we pretend to be.*
Richard Driscoll[21]

Donna sat on the floor in front of my chair, then rose up on her knees and kissed me. I'd been watching her all night at her party. She was tall, blonde, vibrant and obviously loved by everyone in the room. I could also tell that she was older than me, but when we kissed we could have been teenagers. This was beyond all my expectations for the evening and I hadn't even kissed a woman since

---

[21] *You Still Don't Understand.* Driscoll is a therapist dealing with relationship issues, who has some fresh viewpoints on where and for whom gender inequities exist. www.theoppositesex.info

my wife and I had split up a couple of years before, so I was aroused, to say the least. When we sank to the floor and Donna whispered, "No strings attached," that was the biggest turn-on of all.

This was different from any other encounter to date. My pattern had been to approach cautiously, make small talk and assess the prospects from my shy-guy point of view. To have a woman be as direct as this was a shock, but an incredibly pleasant one!

There was no thought of the future in either of our minds as we gave ourselves up to the passion of the moment. I certainly had no idea that this was just the beginning of a long seduction by Donna, a seduction that would hold me in her spotlight, bathe me in her attention and save me from myself. Had I known, as we lay there after our madness had passed, what was going to happen, I probably would have run like a rabbit, but I had just had unexpected sex with a wild woman, and I felt like a man again after such a long time alone. I was grateful and flattered and, because I had felt so 'mutual', I had loved what had happened and certainly didn't think of Donna as a 'slut'. I wanted to see her again, despite my fear of commitment.

I had built up my defenses against a hurtful world, living by myself, working physically hard, trying to appear impervious to pain. I certainly wasn't ready to drop my guard and let another woman into my life. Commitment was a trap, and I had the memories and the scars to prove it.

Back in 1991, in a small house in the cloud forest above Honolulu, I awoke to find my wife already sitting up in bed.

"Morning," I mumbled under my night-breath.

"Paul, I need to tell you something."

That should have woken me up, but I was still drowsy.

"Mm-hmm."

## Paul: Seduction

"I'm in love with you," she said in a meaningful way that went completely unheard. I responded as many a Guy does when confronted like this, "Love you too, babe."

"No, no, no," she said, and this time she aspirated heavily because she always had trouble pronouncing words beginning with H. "I'm in love with Hhhugh."

Well, I did the inappropriate thing — I laughed. What can I say? I like word games and this struck me as funny.

Who was Hugh? He was our neighbor at the time. A nice guy to watch the World Series with, and apparently so much more than that.

So, the laughter subsided and we began the swift disintegration of our fourteen-year relationship. I say that, even though I now know that when faced with the imminent collapse of a marriage, most men will say they didn't see it coming. Although I think of that terribly sad and funny moment as the beginning of the end, it was of course the culmination of years of neglect of our partnership.

During our time together we had lived through some adventures and some hardships, but in the end we were just coasting. Both she and I were dissatisfied, I with myself and she with me. We were going through the habitual motions, and I certainly was not taking an active part in changing that. I think she probably had tried to snap us out of it, but I was too asleep to notice. No wonder she felt the need to look for something – anything – elsewhere.

She left, and I went through a couple of years of spiraling downwards into self-pity and blame. It felt like the ultimate rejection. She had rejected me, and I was rejecting myself. Fortunately, our mutual friends were still around and were a constant support, which kept me from going off the deep end. I was good at putting on my party face, but when I was alone, I was depressed and lonely. I wrote short stories that seemed like the work of a literary genius and added them to my stockpile of earlier work.

Then, one evening, Jack Daniels and I set fire to all of it. In a movie, that moment would have been a turning point, but it wasn't. I just kept going, working at remodeling houses during the day and feeling sorry for myself all night. Then some neighbor friends acquired a ranch in California and cared enough to invite me to help them renovate the ranch house. That was to be the turning point, which brought me to Donna and a new life.

## THE MALE MASK

I think most men have the uneasy feeling that our masculinity, our protection against the world, is under constant threat and we have to guard it at all times. I think in the backs of men's minds we recognize it as a mask, not the real thing. And we worry that it's too thin to protect us from harm. We wish it could be like Darth Vader's helmet — an impenetrable, intimidating protection for the scarred, mask-dependent (and kind of pudgy) man inside — but we fear it's more like an eggshell.

Some of the behavior traits men share and which go into the formation of the Male Mask, are genetic, handed down since apehood. But most of them are taught to us by our parents, teachers and culture. There is no great conspiracy to this, it's how those mentors were raised and how their parents and mentors before them were raised, so it's just one of those things that is perpetuated down the generations. We hope that one of the effects of our book will be that mentors and parents will learn to appreciate and nurture the Feminine as well as the Masculine traits in boys; the full spectrum of human traits, rather than 'boy' and 'girl' traits.[22] There is no doubt that boys and girls behave differently, but the

---

[22] Dan Kindlon & Michael Thompson, *Raising Cain: Protecting the Emotional Life of Boys*. Ballantine, 2000.

suppression of the Feminine in boys has evolutionary ramifications. Carmen McNeil, a college professor of psychology of women, told us at a workshop that when her 3-year-old son has a serious question about life, she asks him, "What does your intuition tell you?" He always has an answer, and he is learning to listen to his innate Feminine. Meanwhile, most men cope with their 'traditional' upbringing.

As we grew up, we were taught that boys don't feel pain, that it's OK for us to hit things with other things, to wrestle and fight, to resolve everything physically — all the boy stuff. That early learning doesn't go away; it's always there at the foundation of our personalities. For some men, it remains their defining characteristic, their way of dealing with the world around them. The conditioning continues through our early years, and as we get older we may retreat into the comfort of the male pattern (unless our mothers and partners teach us otherwise), because it serves as a familiar uniform for us.

Human brains form connections in childhood that establish neural pathways, a network of connections, which become habits and preferred choices.[23] That's part of the struggle all humans, female and male, have with changes to our comfort zones, and it's a large part of the difficulty in forming relationships. The preference is to stay with the known, even at the expense of maturing, and even though women prefer social stability. Most men don't like to stand out in the crowd, we're just guys like the rest of the guys; we're part of the guy team, a brotherhood against the emotional world of the female, the unknown, the gay, the 'weak', the foreign and the mindful.

By the time the cascade of testosterone floods boys' teenage bodies, we are fully entrenched in being guys. We have our instructions

---

[23] Lewis, Amini and Lannon, *A General Theory of Love*, p160

imprinted on our brains. Here's the guys' version of "The List," the instructions that are passed on to most men by culture and are basically unknown, misinterpreted or romanticized by women:

## Cultural Instructions for Being a Guy

- **Don't show emotions** — being too happy or afraid and talking about love is for wimps. The only emotions allowed are expressed during sporting events and if they're necessary *to get sex*.

- **Don't show weakness** — or anything that might be interpreted as weakness by a jury of your peers. It is not manly, it invites bullying and it sets a bad example to the younger boys. It may only be used as a ploy *to get sex*.

- **Be independent** — asking for help is for kids. That includes asking for directions, unless it's a way *to get sex*.

- **Don't admit to needing love or relationship** — save the touchy-feely stuff for Mom, and only on her birthday. The only exception is when using it *to get sex*.

- **Don't let a woman tie you down** — commitment is a noose, it leads to marriage, children and all those inhibiting things preventing men from being the heroic figures they ought to be. The only time for docility is if it *leads to sex*.

- **Don't show pain** — grit your teeth, steel your spine, set your jaw, squint your eyes. Pain means nothing, even the pain of rejection. Carry on as if nothing can hurt you, unless you're *looking for sympathy sex*.

## Fight or Flee

Part of the Male Mask's usefulness is for survival in this dangerous world of ours. It's the shield from behind which we scan our surroundings, whenever we're away from our home base. We step out of our front doors, no matter if we live in a New York apartment or an Idaho farmhouse, and what's the first thing most men do? They scan for trouble. They look around, along the corridor, across the yard, up and down the street, whatever. They may not actually stop and look. They may not give any sign that they're scanning. They probably don't even realize they're doing it, but they are. A man walking down a city street is probably unconsciously attuned and aware of what's going on around him. It's instinctual to most men, perhaps because of the hunting history of mankind.

All that scanning goes on behind the Male Mask, which hides the fact that we're aware and ready to fight or flee at any time. We men do such a good job of hiding it that most women don't realize how attentive we are to the world around us, because we look so relaxed, or bored or annoyed that we're being dragged from store to store. Women may see the physical signs of our emotions, but might not pick up on the constant background tension we experience outside our comfort zone of home.

So that's the false front that women have to understand when they get involved with men. Most women believe men's Masks to be our real selves and think we're always in control, coolly navigating our way through our lives. No upsets, no fears, no threats to our steely exterior.

When we men find ourselves in a stable relationship, we may feel safe enough with our partners that we allow the Male Mask to slip when we're with them. Suddenly we're confronted by our real selves, and we may not like it all that much. We're naturally, and that means biologically, gun-shy about the concept of commitment at the beginning of a relationship anyway, so any unmasking is doubly threatening.

## How It's Meant to Be

So here we are, average guys hiding ourselves behind our Mask, guarding against ridicule and rejection, radiating strength and confidence, and hoping that nobody makes us have to prove ourselves. The great thing about a true partnership with a woman—once we've got over the initial fear, dropped the Mask, seen our true selves and realized that this isn't such a bad deal after all—is that we can relax around our partner. We can take off this restrictive bloody Mask and, at least with her, we can be real. It's all about being **comfortable**, secure enough in her company to let our guard down and enjoy true companionship. That's just about all she wants too, although there will be some baggage to go with the arrangement.

But think about it — until a man is in a true partnership, the only people with whom he doesn't have to pretend to be someone he isn't are his parents, at least while he is still at home. There is a lot of posturing around parents as we grow up, but once we have left the nest we only show our real selves around the women we live with. That can be scary, but it can also be a great relief.

In my case, I always felt loved and protected in my English childhood home. But when I reflect on how much my parents knew about me, I believe I was more a generic child to them than an individual. The generic "good child" was the perfect English child; no fuss or bother, with perfect table manners and politeness, set on a reliable course towards a respectable future regardless of individual skills and traits. (Of course this was itself a mask wrought of centuries of patriarchal culture, preparing me for my own version of the Male Mask.) Children's opinions were not to be expressed in public; conversation at home was limited to commercial breaks on evening television.

Later, despite my non-conformist appearance and lifestyle, I continued to wear the "good child" mask (albeit a good child with a thirst for sex and other rush-inducing pursuits), until I entered my first long-term relationship. Only then did I begin to let it drop. And it has only been since meeting Donna in my 40s, that I have been able to fully expose and examine the real Paul and his history in the safety that men find in the company of the partner they love.

Do women know that they have the power to unmask us? I think they have an inkling of it, but mostly they don't consider it a real strength, since it has been denigrated for so long. That's why we wrote this book — to give men and women some practical help in getting together and knowing more about what makes each other tick.

## Shared Responsibility

Donna and I believe that Western women have never really known their own feminine power, and have been unable to live up to the biological partnership they are meant to have with the men in their lives. Patriarchal culture frowned on too much feminine influence in boys' upbringing. The female half of our species has forgotten how to teach men to expand ourselves and to take off the Male Mask with those we care for.

So there's a portion of the responsibility for the state of the patriarchal world to be laid on women as well as men.[24] Women gave up their power to men long ago and now we're all reaping the harvest of that mistake. We are all victims of the loss of the Functional Feminine in cultures worldwide.

The conditions that women in many cultures are living under are unfathomably cruel. And in some cases, such as the genital mutilation of girls that is often carried out by female relatives of the victim, the cruelty continues with the consent of the disempowered women of previous generations.[25] It's an extreme proof of the loss of

---

[24] Felicia Pratto, *Sex, Power, Conflict*, quoted in *Standup Guy* by Michael Segell, p121

[25] Mary Daly, *Gyn/Ecology: The Metaethics of Radical Feminism*, Beacon Press 1978. World Health Organization, Fact Sheet No. 241, February 2010

the Functional Feminine and the tyranny of the Dysfunctional Masculine.

It will take more than his book to stop such widespread horrors. But we must begin somewhere, and the western cultures still set many examples for the rest of the world. We believe the change can only start when individual women begin to act in functional ways and set examples that will inspire other women. That's why *Seduction Redefined* is promoting a partnership revolution, starting with women learning to assert themselves in a relationship. It's good for them, it's great for men and in the long run, it will change the world for the better, and, who knows, it might even make war and other atrocities unpopular with men!

# CHAPTER THREE

## Donna: Selection

### *Ladies' Choice – Women Seeking and Selecting*

*One of the core powers of feminine seduction is to remind a man of all the different varieties of masculinity that can be attractive to a woman. Every act of seduction asks for a certain response from a man.* Geoffrey Miller[26]

While seeking 'a Paul', I think I talked with at least twenty men through personal classifieds, met with four or five and asked twenty thousand questions, mostly on the telephone. My 'psychic sifter', the part of my brain that silently sorts all the information I receive, sent up flares on smaller issues and then rockets when it came to a conclusion. It was so simple, it revealed that I simply wanted a responsible, sensuous lover with intelligence and humor. With Paul, I got much more.

---

[26] Interviewed for Baring Witness. www.BaringWitnessFilm.org

Launch, launching, launched. My psyche and body was ready. In walks Paul. The personals had been very educational and fun and each telephone call had been part of the learning curve for all parties.

One day a neighbor wanted me to introduce a newcomer to the community. I finally found the time to leave him a message and invited him to a local Open Mic Night. He came and asked for me and we had several friendly words and that was it. No love at first sight. He came to the next Open Mic too. Thus far, my world was not shaken by the six-foot-four, golden Englishman, but about three weeks later, after inviting neighbors and Paul to a potluck pasta party in my art studio, my universe exploded.

He did four things right:

- The Number One great thing he did to bring his homemade bread and tabouleh.

- Number Two was he washed the dishes - (too good to be true!)

- Number Three and most mysterious, he stayed, after almost everyone had left, to talk in front of the fire. That's when I discovered a friendly, drop-dead stunning smile and a superb, intelligent sense of humor.

- Number Four? You know....No Strings Attached!

Paul walked into my life with the right mystical sexual chemistry. The first powerful dynamic of our coupling was my being an Alpha and he a Beta, which immediately created a power balance in my favor and made my Alpha Female seduction of him much easier. He has no issues about 'feeling like a man', because he is so secure in his masculinity. Physically, we are both very tall, with spotty, sun-damaged skin and just the right number of wrinkles.

From my experience, most guys don't have the experience and maturity to become mindful, malleable men until they are forty or so. They then slow down, are more willing to share and are more prone to deep listening. So, even though we still hear from frustrated single women that most attractive men appear to be either married, 'mashers' or gay, there are not only millions of available, if immature, young men, but also millions of mature, attractive men, mostly living alone, all wandering around waiting for companionship – with YOU!

My decision to say "no strings attached", my willingness to be the seducer, make almost all the calls (which by the way could be labeled 'phone sex' using my breathy voice), were all intuitive strokes of genius on my part. I made him comfortable and I chose someone who was to become my loving, amazing life partner!

## Darwin, You and I

Little did I know, when I set out to seduce Paul, that my intuitive skills were a product of evolution that could hold the key to ending the gender wars and changing patriarchy to partnership.

Charles Darwin is best known for his theory of Natural Selection, one tenet of which, the survival of the fittest, gave rise to so-called Social Darwinism. Politicians, scientists and other powerful men latched onto 'Survival of the Fittest', and they used it to provide them with some scientific backing for their discriminatory ideological doctrine, seeking to justify immoral social inequality between classes, races and sexes.

Ironically, in *The Descent of Man, and Selection in Relation to Sex*, Darwin wrote only twice of "survival of the fittest" but wrote of "love" ninety-five times![27]

Darwin studied animal behavior and the preening and posturing that males do around females and each other. He realized that most

---

[27] David Loye, *Darwin's Lost Theory*. Founder of the Darwin Project, Loye seeks to correct the suppression of the real teachings of Darwin, such as the "survival of the fittest" meme that was used to excuse imperialism and slavery.

of the variations in plumage, coloring, sexual organs, and behavior of males of all species were created and preserved through the selection of those attributes by females. In particular, Darwin wondered about the seemingly useless qualities and traits in animal species, such as extravagant plumage and mating displays, and why they existed at the expense of the energy and safety of the males.

His theory of Sexual Selection proposed that the traits displayed by the males existed only because generations of females had desired and selected for them in the mating process. In short, mate choice by females was a major factor in determining the evolution of the species.

Darwin applied the hypothesis to humans in writing *The Descent of Man*. Far from being heralded as the revolutionary work it was, the theory was dismissed by the male scientific establishment of the time, because it was so ridiculous to think that females of any species, especially women, could have any such powers of discernment and taste, or could choose which males were to be their mates. Darwin himself held the prevailing Victorian attitudes toward women and his social prejudices existed alongside his revolutionary theory, *which was neglected for a century*,[28] when evolutionists began to take a new look at his work.

In the 1980s, evolutionary biologists began to document the sexual selection tactics used by women.[29] While the competition between males is still important, the selection of mates by females was finally recognized as equally,[30] if not more important, especially since those

---

[28] Geoffrey Miller, *The Mating Mind*, p.33: Miller here explains the tortured history of Darwin's theory as it was discussed and discarded for a century.

[29] David M. Buss, 1994; Sarah Blaffer Hrdy, 1999; Geoffrey Miller, 2001.

[30] Patricia Gowaty, 1992

choices could be conscious ones, rather than passive, luck-of-the-draw outcomes.[31]

The male peacock's tail and the man's noisy motorcycle are open displays of what they hope are 'desirable' masculine traits, even though both the tail and the bike pose survival risks: the tail being cumbersome enough to prevent escape from a predator and the bike being at the mercy of the rider's own faculties. Not to mention the willingness of the man to inflict painful noise pollution on everyone and every species around him to prove something, perhaps to himself, about his masculinity.

Females of their respective species must choose whether or not the extravagant show of their suitors is proof of genetic superiority worthy to be passed onto their offspring. A gaudy tail might show genetic strength, but a painfully loud motorcycle...? Is that the kind of trait you need to encourage? Will this man father the kind of offspring the world needs?

Who knows what damage has been inflicted on him in his life, that this should be his display? We see him as a victim of the runaway Alpha-Mask culture, not to be blamed, but, if there should be an attraction to him, to be guided to find the real man within; the unmasked Functional Masculine that the world really needs.

## A Brave New Idea

This is a brave new idea for women — that we can be the instigators of relationship, and you can do it without blaming men for their biologically driven actions, which are only displays designed to attract us. Men might think they will attract us because that's what

---

[31] Griet Vandermassen, *Sexual Selection: A Tale of Male Bias and Feminist Denial*, 2004. An article in which Dr Vandermassen explains sexual selection, discusses male bias in and feminist reaction to the theory and demonstrates the loss for feminist understanding of gender differences in continuing to reject the evolutionary framework.

the male dominator culture has taught them and our foremothers would not, or were not allowed to, choose otherwise. It's a proof of how far we have strayed from our biological roles that formed our species over hundreds of millennia! We women have for too long been passive observers.

In most societies worldwide, willingly or not, men have also taken on the awesome burden of initiating and trying to control relationship while women have been trained to succumb without question. From ancient times, marriages arranged by men became the instruments for business or power-brokering needs and the all-male priesthood created the rituals and rules of contact, all of which contributed to a loss of faith in the Feminine and thereby the undervaluing of women.

*It is the female over and over again who selects the one who appeals to her...and that concept was resisted in science until relatively late in the 20th century as a further proof of the male bias infecting science and infecting the whole society.* David Loye[32]

## Beta Baboons Rule!

The good news is we need only look to Nature, as Darwin did, for enlightenment. The possibility of a cultural shift from Alpha-Male-dominated to Beta-friendly is shown by a troop of wild baboons in Kenya whose aggressive, dominant males were wiped out by bovine tuberculosis in tainted meat that they had fought each other to obtain and had kept the females and subordinate males from eating.

The troop suddenly went from being a typical baboon society of aggression by dominant males against females and subordinate

---

[32] www.davidloye.com

males to one in which there was far less violence, more tolerance and more peaceful grooming behavior.[33]

Remarkably, although there was a normal influx of adolescent males from other troops in search of mates, these suitors learned and conformed to the behavior of the troop. Thus, the behavior persisted and after twenty years, when none of the survivors of the illness remained alive, the troop is still a peaceful, conciliatory, tolerant society with a relaxed form of hierarchy. Tests of the baboons' hormone levels have shown a marked lowering of stress, even in low-ranking males.

After the disease had killed off the aggressive males, there were twice as many females as males, and the males were the Betas of the original troop. The females were friendlier to each other (and to the remaining and the incoming males) without the stress of many dominant males competing violently over them and acting aggressively towards them. The skewed ratio of female to male has persisted to the present, along with the relatively peaceful atmosphere of the troop.

So the influence of the Feminine, in the absence of runaway over-aggressiveness by male dominators, has helped create a society in which violent behavior is discouraged and is unattractive to females in estrus. Their prospective mates learn to be less violent in order to partner with them. All of which is "abnormal" for their species. So take heart and believe that even our entrenched behaviors can be altered. Males are supremely adaptable to female preferences.

## Startling Stats

Now let's give you a realistic courtship perspective, something else that goes completely against what we have been taught: Of men

---

[33] Robert Sapolsky, Lisa Share, A Pacific Culture among Wild Baboons: Its Emergence and Transmission, PLoS Biology Journal, April 2004.

who want to be in a relationship, only 2% put physical beauty at the top of their list of needs. This is from a well-known international study, published in 1989 by Professor David Buss[34]. The researchers asked men and women which qualities they would prefer in their mate.

Apart from the obvious desire for mutual attraction, would you like to guess what was top of the list for both men and women? Kindness, dependability, emotional stability and health, all qualities that lead to a feeling of security and comfort with someone. Above beauty and status. In fact, good looks took *tenth place* for men and thirteenth for women. Ponder that for a moment.

That doesn't mean that physical beauty, youth and health aren't genetically hardwired into the male sexual fantasy (women's, too!), but men who want to *stay* with women look beyond physical beauty and go for how comfortable they are: the man you choose simply needs to be given the chance to get to know the real woman you are in order to overcome his raw, media-titillated desires.

It's men's role to display their traits so women can choose from among them. But since human males don't have the extravagant plumage or brightly colored body parts that other species have developed for courting, they display the qualities that they *think* women want to see in a mate. These could be machismo or sensitivity, wealth or asceticism, physical prowess or mental creativity, stoicism or excitability. It's ladies' choice!

So how much of this display is real and how much only for show? That can only be judged through the weeding process, which includes the use of seduction by a woman to make a man comfortable enough to lower his Mask to show the woman his real

---

[34] D.M. Buss, *Sex Differences in Human Mate Selection: Evolutionary Hypotheses Tested in 37 Cultures*: Men and women want something more in a mate than good hair and expensive jewelry. Don't tell the authors of *The Rules*!

self. Seduction is an essential tool for every woman who desires a lasting relationship, and every woman has what it takes to be a seductress. Just remember that your Perfect Man may not exist except in your mind, and since everyone's idea of perfection is different, it's up to you to guide your choice of partner in that direction. Seduction is the key and it's on your key-ring!

And you won't be entirely alone in selecting your partner. There are still a few places in the world where it has long been an accepted part of the culture for women to choose their mates. In the Bijagos Archipelago off the West African coast, for example, the women propose to their chosen partners with plates of fish and long-lived partnerships have been the norm. Now, however, Christian missionaries and other outside influences are changing all that, and divorce rates are rising there as traditions become more westernized.

## Make a Selection Trait List

Sit down and make a list of attributes you desire in a man. Once you clarify in your mind what your wants and what your real needs are, you will stand a better chance of finding someone who has at least some of the more realistic traits. It is far better to understand your motives at the beginning than to try to figure them out later, when you may be in an unsatisfying or even abusive relationship. The longer you wait to recognize a bad choice, the harder it is to extricate yourself.

With the wisdom and simplicity of later life, the needs that led me to Paul were only two - a sense of humor and the ability to write poetry. That's not to say I wasn't looking for someone attractive and about the same height, but really those were added bonuses. Your wish list will probably be longer. Start out with a list of everything you want and everything you need, then go through it and be a stern editor. It might help to put numbers on a scale of one to five alongside each entry, so now the entry that says "Must have big feet" will probably rank lower than "Must like children".

This is really a way of focusing your intention, of making your search real. But you must be flexible and not expect Mr. Perfect to appear as if by magic, just because you've made a list. Flexibility of priorities is important, since you may meet someone interesting, but who doesn't have enough check marks on your list. If your intuition is telling you to take a chance, take a chance! Just stay in the Now.

Now go back through the list and prioritize those priorities again. Pretty soon, you'll have whittled the list of main priorities down to a handful. From there, you can see which are wants and which are true needs. The difference is up to you, since needs are so personal. "Must be a Red Sox fan" could be either a want or a need, depending on how rabid a fan you are; "Must have a penis" is a little more universal, but it may not be all that important to you. Or, if you only want a brief affair rather than anything serious and sustained, or just a one-night stand this time around, your priorities will be less stringent.

You can really be spontaneous and see what happens, as I did. Who knows, you might meet your own version of Paul by taking the chance. Stay in the Now, don't encumber yourself or him with your expectations, be open to serendipity and synchronicity. Keep your list in the back of your mind and be alert to the possibility that whomever you meet might be a candidate for seduction in the long-term.

Just be as realistic as possible about your needs, because they are what will decide what kind of partner you'll be seeking. Don't expect the entire package to turn up on your doorstep, in the shape of your Ideal Man with no flaws.

Remember that kindness will help you to find the precious qualities hidden behind his Mask. Use your intuition as well and have some fun - after all, seduction is meant to be enjoyable for both of you. Empower yourself with the innate Feminine biological wisdom to select your partner.

# CHAPTER FOUR

## Paul: Selection

### *Men Display and Women Select*

*Evolutionary biologists think of men as a vast breeding experiment run by women, because everything we do in relation to them, and often with and to each other, provides clues to our desirability as mates.*
Michael Segell, *Standup Guy*.

Never in a million years would I have had the wisdom to know that Donna was exactly what I needed – the perfect selection for me! Donna knew what she wanted and also saw in me someone that I didn't even suspect was there.

When I first met Donna, I was unconscious to the fact that my life was a burned-out hulk of what it had been. I had sunk pretty low following the break-up of my marriage. I don't know how my body stood the grief and the booze. I could have sought help from a therapist, but I can't remember even considering that, being a big, tough, self-sufficient guy and all. I had friends who kept me occupied and feeling loved, which felt good, but I had no real outlet for my pain, so I kept it inside. I needed more than to simply look for sex with the available women I met. Without knowing it, I was eager, like most men, to have a woman listen to me, comfort me, encourage me and just take me in her arms.

Donna did all that for me, and more. But, being in the manly mode, with my Male Mask firmly in place, I was too wrapped up in my own misery at first to appreciate what she was doing for me. I was more intent on suffering stoically the pain I had brought upon myself. Later, I recognized that Donna was just the person I needed to bring me back to life with her amazing insight into what was missing in me.

Our partnership has opened me up enough to be able to examine myself and my life up to this point, something that I would have shied away from in my earlier, less conscious years. Donna's nurturing instinct, her constant fascination in the human condition and her passion for increasing awareness couldn't help but rub off on me, hence my involvement in this book.

I discovered that what I needed from a relationship was a partnership that would allow me to be myself, with someone who appreciated my better qualities and was willing to work without blame on my worse ones. What that means is that she is able to see the roots of my failings in the lack of 'education' or training I received in the past, when I was pretty much going it alone. In that way, I'm not made to feel that I am to blame for not knowing instinctively how to be the best partner she could have.

Donna has given me the freedom to choose how I live my life, while offering me the chance to partake of her interests. I've chosen to get involved more in her projects, which have become collaborations, and less in my full-time construction business. Like most men, I needed to feel wanted and to feel that my choices were open. That way, I could retain at least a semblance of independence, while helping accomplish the collaboration that is so important to partnership.

Part of the joy of active partnership, apart from the freely available sex, of course, is the respect it brings, especially in a *creative collaboration* such as ours. So, while both of us have an irreverent sense of humor, and almost no subject is sacred, we avoid public put-downs. That means Donna allows me to wear my Male Mask in the world and I can allow myself to take a back seat to her in areas where she is more knowledgeable or skilful than I. We know we both have our own strengths and we honor them in each other and augment them.

## Selection and the Male Mask

Because it's partly biological, partly cultural, we men don't have much choice in how we wear the Male Mask until women come along to teach us other ways. It exists partly because women selected men thousands of years ago with the genuine traits the Mask tries to exhibit to the world; the coolness under pressure, the bravery, extreme focus and self-assuredness of the pure Alpha. The Male Mask that hides most men's lack of these qualities is an essential part of men's survival toolkit. So the Mask has become the cultural norm and men are taught to construct it from an early age.

The Mask is very useful for the pilot of the passenger jet with an engine on fire and the lifeboat skipper rescuing sailors in a storm. It emanates the emotional detachment and calm-under-fire veneer that helps others survive dangerous situations. Women understand and desire that part of us. But applied to everyday life and a budding relationship, it's an emotional hurdle for a partner to overcome. And it's the quintessential male display.

Since the 1970s, Darwin's theory of Sexual Selection has become a subject of debate among academicians in biology, evolutionary psychology and cultural anthropology. Researchers are discovering that almost everything we take for granted about our society, including our Male Masks, was created as a form of sexual display by men so that we would be selected for mating by women. That can include complex language, art, music, writing, religion, science

– on and on – and that's in addition to the usual things we associate with masculinity, like competition, war and hunting.

## Displaying

Hunting for large game, by the way, was always partly about courtship display. It turns out that it's usually the women in contemporary hunter-gatherer societies that supply most of the family food, with the meat portion mostly derived from trapping small animals. The likelihood is that this was common to all hunter-gatherer societies, even prehistoric societies from which all humans originate.

Men go off hunting bigger animals, with great show of the bravery of leaving family and hearth in dangerous pursuit of nourishment, and come back with nothing at least ninety per cent of the time[35]. Not a very reliable source of food for the family. When they do manage to kill a large animal, they have to divide it up among many people so it can be eaten before it rots.

The act of hunting therefore was more of a display of physical fitness and of kindness through the act of altruism of sharing among the tribe[36]. Those traits are desired by the women in their society, and that's why these men continue to spend so much time chasing after animals and not catching them, or giving them away when they do catch them. A University of Utah analysis found that if hunting were truly about the efficiency of gaining food, men would give up their bows and guns and become full-time gatherers.[37] It's certainly less about efficiency than it is about displaying intelligence and bravery, getting away from the wife for a

---

[35] Geoffrey Miller, *The Mating Mind*, p309

[36] *Ibid*, p311

[37] Robert Boyd & Joan B. Silk, *How Humans Evolved*, p.637

while and reinforcing their bonds with the rest of the men. This was what we did before football.

One of the ongoing debates in evolutionary psychology has been about the "selfish gene" viewpoint, in which altruism, the selfless concern for the well-being of others, would be counter-intuitive as a mating strategy, while self-preservation would be paramount. David Buss' and others' findings[38] show that selflessness is an important attractor for women. As Geoffrey Miller wrote, we don't talk on a first date about all the selfish, rude or unkind things we might have done. We would be more likely to talk about our acts of kindness to others, even though these acts have no obvious personal benefit and may even be dangerous. Miller believes altruism and moral behavior are direct results of sexual selection.[39] Kindness is sexy!

Sharing the spoils is also a chance for men to form strong bonds of trust with their fellow men and also to maintain their respective places in the hierarchy; the strategists and the followers, the marksmen and the beaters, the trackers and the carriers, the fastest and the slowest. But even male hierarchies have a lot to do with impressing prospective mates, so it's not so much about survival as it is about getting selected!

So, females are major drivers of evolution and, by virtue of their ability to choose men's desirable heritable traits, women are the potential saviors of our species. The problem is, when they are not allowed to make the choices, or if those choices are limited to traits that are undesirable, the species may develop primarily those traits that threaten its survival, usually through male-to-male conflict.

---

[38] Tim Phillips (2008), *The evolution of human altruism towards non-kin through sexual selection*. University of Nottingham. Pat Barclay (2010) *Altruism as a courtship display*, British Journal of Psychology.

[39] Geoffrey Miller, *The Mating Mind*, p. 292

## We Are Victims of Our Own Runaway Traits

It's our hypothesis that this is what's happening to our own species. *We are victims of the runaway selection of what our culture has conditioned us to consider desirable masculine traits.* The peacock's tail seems an appropriate metaphor for the state of our species, in which the choices made have created mating displays whose effects endanger us all. Researchers looking for evidence of Sexual Selection investigate behavior and indicators that are costly in every area but may improve a male's chance of being selected as a mate and thus the reproduction of his genes. Hence the usual example of the peacock's tail – useless and dangerous in every way except for courtship display as a sign of his genetic health. It has no other purpose and may even get the peacock killed when he can't make a quick getaway from predators.[40]

So it is with most human (statistically speaking, male) inventions that don't have a direct connection with survival, like conspicuous over-consumption, acquisition of wealth, loud things, complicated language, sports, art, technical innovation, war, science, Jet Skis. They're all about us strutting our stuff in front of women, who then choose which qualities they wish their mates and offspring to have.

When there are no limiting factors on mating behaviors, such as the danger of predation or the depletion of energy, they will become **runaway traits**. A newly discovered example of that is a tiny European insect called the water boatman, which produces the loudest sound produced by an animal, when adjusted for its size.[41] Apparently, these flea-sized insects have no predators that find

---

[40] Charles Darwin, *The Descent of Man*, p415

[41] Jérôme Sueur, David Mackie, James Windmill; *So Small, So Loud: Extremely High Sound Pressure Level from a Pygmy Aquatic Insect (Corixidae, Micronectinae)*. PLoS ONE 6(6): e21089. June 15, 2011.

them via their call. Since there is no risk to making a loud sound to attract female attention, the males have been recorded making a 99-decibel chirping sound by vibrating their penises. (The legal limit for a motorcycle exhaust in the U.S. is 81 decibels!)

Females will select the males who create the best display for them. Male displays will become more pronounced and exaggerated until a limiting factor manifests itself, such as self-annihilation in the human race's case, but until then, they will continue to adapt to the female preference.

Knowing that, we start to get an inkling of how powerful is women's influence on men and how fundamental their selection of desired traits is in human development. And we realize that the strong Male Mask we learn to wear as we mature is mostly for the benefit of what women in the past wanted in their men. In the 1990 study by David Buss, women in thirty-seven cultures around the world were asked to list their priorities in potential mates. After "mutual attraction" they listed traits like *kindness, dependability, maturity* and *emotional stability,* which together form a good template for a basic Male Mask.

## Is That Me?

So the Male Mask is a natural phenomenon, part of the courtship display and created by women's desires and exacerbated by patriarchy. Most cultures, and certainly all "developed" cultures, are patriarchies, which have tended to advance men's aspirations, often at the expense of women.[42] That has affected our Male Masks, to the point where the basic foundation — dependability, maturity, emotional stability — can be hidden under layers of machismo,

---

[42] Gerda Lerner, The Creation of Patriarchy, p.43

egocentricity, greed and aggression, which the psychologist Hans Eysenck calls *psychoticism*.[43]

## Paul's Tale of How Patriarchy Came to Be

We need women to select and to guide men into partnership. After researching for this book I've formed a hypothesis concerning early human history and the formation of patriarchies.

Women were going about their business of providing food for their families, perhaps growing some, gathering the rest and trapping small animals. At the same time they were taking care of the children, carrying the young ones and nurturing the others.

Then there were the men, protecting the family from danger and going off hunting larger animals, but failing most of the time. They'd come back tired and bad-tempered and get in the way of the women preparing the evening meal. Since this was before Fox News and The Sports Channel, the women would encourage them to go do something to get them out of the cave. So the men would gather in their separate men's area and commiserate over the failed hunt.

Pretty soon, they'd get to other subjects and their increasing brain size (a trait that exists partly because it was selected for by their foremothers) would allow them to imagine things. That was something new in the world - imagination. It wouldn't take long before they'd come up with some pretty good excuses for a failed hunt, like "the gods were angry."

They'd go home and tell their women about the hunting god they'd invented. The women, tired after a long day of keeping the family alive, would mumble something like "Yeah, whatever."

That encouraged the men to carry on imagining. Before long, they imagined that they weren't getting enough respect from the

---

[43] Hans Eysenck, *The definition and measurement of psychoticism*, Personality & Individual Differences,

women, that they needed laws. Then they created religions with gods to give the laws some divine meaning that the women also had to believe in. So the snowball got rolling. Before the women knew what was really going on, the men were imposing their invented laws, customs and religions on them, along with severe restrictions and punishments for women that spoke out against them. Remember, these guys were armed and indignant, a lethal combination. So the women, to keep life quiet and so they could go on doing their nurturing thing, went along with the whole deal, not realizing what it would all mean to their distant descendants.

So patriarchies were formed, wars were fought with neighboring patriarchies, men became more violently aggressive towards everyone and everything and began to feel they were meant to be that way, and women became powerless, all because they relinquished their power at a critical moment.

### Listen to the Feminine

Was it that simple? Probably not, but the way men behave when no-one's around to tell us different gives us some insight into how patriarchy might have been created. But we are also designed to listen and learn from the women in our lives, who can help us pay attention to the feminine side of our own nature - the side that enables us to be loving husbands and fathers, that allows us to be humane and caring about others and to help in forming and sustaining community.[44]

When we find ourselves in a stable relationship, we can feel safe enough with our partners that we allow the Male Mask to slip when we're with them. Suddenly we're confronted by our real selves, and we may not like it all that much. We're naturally, and that means biologically, gun-shy about the concept of commitment at the beginning of a relationship anyway, so the unmasking is doubly

---

[44] Jeremy Rifkin, *The Empathic Civilization*. Tarcher/Penguin 2009

threatening. Yet it is a necessary threat to the Alpha-mask culture that pervades politics, business and everyday life.

Cultural evolution will only occur, we believe, when women understand the restrictions they have lived with that go beyond unequal pay and corporate glass ceilings, the right to vote and the right to choose what grows in their wombs. The worst restrictions are the ones that discourage women from understanding their functional feminine strengths. There is a shift happening, but too often, in our opinion, it is cloaked in quasi-religious, masculine terms of divinity and the soul. These are terms that men created for their own religious ends, which they can understand and which Alpha-Mask men know how to subvert and challenge.

Talk about innate intuition and most men cannot relate. Speak of the serene knowledge of their life-giving nature that women possess at their core, and most men will be silent. Women understand these things inherently, whether they articulate them or not. They are part of what makes women so mysterious and unnerving to men, and which drove men to create their runaway dominator cultures and religions.

When women become more aware of the functional Feminine and begin to listen to their intuition in the choices they make, then change can take place that just might help our species survive. That change will come when the Feminine and Masculine combine their strengths in partnership, when the female and male brains become two distinct parts of the same, human, brain.

As women begin to seek out more overtly the Male Displays of openness, kindness and dependability, men will be in a position to be less masked and will feel safe in their mindfulness.

# CHAPTER FIVE

## Donna: Initiating

### *Women Initiating – Overcoming Fear*

*First and foremost,* Woman *must emerge from the woman. She must become aware of what she really is, and she must integrate that awareness into the way she views herself and the world, as it becomes part and parcel of her life.*
André van Lysebeth, *Tantra: The Cult of the Feminine*

In my small town, I felt completely at ease with Paul. I had talked with him at a couple of previous meetings, had watched him at my party and trusted friends had introduced him to me in the first place. Yes, we had a couple of glasses of wine during the evening with dinner, but we all know that sometimes a little alcohol helps our fear of rejection and gives us the edge of courage.

To say it again, men are EVERYWHERE and they are not all mashers, gay, married, maimed, perverts or dangerous women-haters. Getting their attention by just showing kindness, by simply speaking to them, is easy. So then what? Intention opens doors to chance, fate, luck, magic, God's grace. "God helps those who help themselves." Intention made me stand straight, smile more and feel alive: in other words, I felt like a Woman!

My self-esteem was intact, even though it was difficult at times with Paul when I knew I would have to be the one to continue the calling. That was when I would call my dear girlfriends Toni and Barbara for moral support. I was "willing to work" (dress up, cook, drive to his place) for our time spent together. He was generous and giving in everything except initiating, so what was there to whine about? It was working.

I do know that almost any single man is available to you when trust and comfort are established. It was simple with Paul because all I knew was I wanted a poetic, intelligent mindful male with a sense of humor and I got much, much more.

And an encouraging thing to remember if you're seeking a more mature man, is that generally, men over forty are more willing to drop their Male Masks and be more flexible in many ways, because they have succeeded at the 'professional high jump'. They've had more experience of the highs and lows of normal life and have more chance of being more comfortable in themselves.

## The Physical and Psychological Fear Factor

When I was in my twenties, a constant, gnawing, unfriendly voice inside of me kept asking, "What would a man see in me?" and the same little voice said, "I'm too tall, my nose is too long, my lips are too thin, my skin is blotchy and my breasts are too small." The little voice continued, "I am just not an interesting person - even if I do read Time magazine - and nobody wants my opinions anyway. How could I ever find any man interested in me?"

Later in life, my epiphanies about self-esteem began to evolve and I understood that *nobody* is perfect and *everybody* has insecurities and varying degrees of **low self-esteem** – it's endemic to the human race. Remember that **body shame** is a cultural norm, especially for women. That means everybody you admire for their looks, their talents, their bravery, their wealth - whatever it is about them that you wish you had - everybody thinks they're lacking *something*. The best-looking movie stars see flaws when they look in the mirror. Julia Roberts has said that she looks like she has a coat hanger in her mouth.

Once you really get that, you can feel better about yourself. It worked so well for me that I began the habit of engaging strangers by complimenting them on something they're wearing, or asking cashiers if their backs hurt. It's amazing how people smile and wake from their work-trances with just a few kind, personal words. A revelation for a woman with self-esteem issues!

## Codes For Living

The mass entertainment media and advertising companies have created an artificial culture, producing, in addition to dress codes, a face code, fanny code, waist code, teeth code, hair code, leg code and the big one - breast code. Enough codes! Your new Code for living – is to live! Take action and initiate! The secret to remember is that, although we're taught that all these codes are important if we want to find partners, most men, given the seductive chance to feel safe and comfortable, don't care about any of them enough to turn down a good seduction. Sure, there are certain norms of cleanliness, but beyond that, most men will succumb to kindness and attention.

Because there is *something special* about you - you're a woman, and women are desirable to men. That's why all women in the presence of men assume Alpha status. It's not your looks or brilliant conversation that will mean the most to him, once you have made contact. What is real is how comfortable and safe you make him feel, while still surprising him now and again. If you can show him how safe he is with you, how comfortable he can be in your company and how much fun you can be, you won't be drab to him - you will be warm, fun, authentic and fascinating in his eyes.

## Fatty Deposits (or none) as Beauty

I'm not saying that men don't fantasize about beautiful women. They do, because it's hard-wired in them to be attracted to wide pelvised, large breasted, youthful women to propagate the species. It's an instinctive response to be attracted to prime reproductive females with fatty deposits in the breasts and buttocks. The fatty deposits actually have no real bearing on reproductive fitness, but have evolved because that's what our forefathers desired in women and came to regard as signs of fertility and health.[45] That's sexual selection from the other side.

And yet, we all see the fashion-mag images of bulimic waif models, and generations of girls have played with Anatomically-Impossible Barbie. These also appeal to men, as do the porn stars and dancers many of them fantasize about. You can see that there is no perfect way to look to attract a man, because (and this is a secret!) they don't really know what their perfect woman looks like. The reality of relationship is that men are fearful of Woman with a capital 'W', and after all the fantasies subside, they prefer and need women who display more nurturing qualities - women who can make them **comfortable.**

## THE FIVE GOLDEN MANTRAS THAT REDEFINE SEDUCTION

There are some basic mantras for you to remember to give you the self-confidence you need to initiate a relationship. Right now, as you read them for the first time, spend a little meditative time on each one, so you really get the meanings and the ramifications.

---

[45] Geoffrey Miller, *The Mating Mind*, p.229; Leonard Shlain, *Sex, Time and Power*. Viking, 2003.

Then print them out and put them on your refrigerator, so you'll have a constant reminder.

## 1: WOMEN, NOT MEN, ARE BIOLOGICALLY EQUIPPED TO CHOOSE THEIR PARTNERS.[46]

Your body is a nurturing machine, your brain is wired to respond to need in others, especially your own children, with sympathy and compassion. His body is made to spread seed and his brain is wired for competition. Women are programmed, physically, mentally, spiritually and emotionally, to find the best seed for their eggs and to find a protector, so she can raise healthy offspring in a safe environment.

That's a purely biological view of the human animal. What it means to a twenty first century woman in western culture is that the hardwiring is still there, even if she has no intention of bearing children. That wiring will help you find the best partner. In every way you are the one best equipped to choose. And our bumper sticker "The egg knows more than the sperm" is an expression of that ability. The egg itself creates many obstacles and tests for the sperm in order to select the best among millions.[47] And women are equipped with the intuitive skill to select the most desirable display behaviors and he men displaying them.

### Designed To Choose

*Seduction Redefined* is about being conscious of our powers and abilities, one of which is the ability to bring new humans into the world and the power to choose when that should happen. It is not the man's place to choose when a woman should get pregnant. That is either the woman's choice alone, or a decision made between her

---

[46] Charles Darwin, The Descent of Man.

[47] Sarah Robertson (2009), *Immune regulation of conception and embryo implantation – all about quality control?* Journal of Reproductive Immunology.

and her chosen partner. The politicization of women's bodies by male society has warped our self-image to a point where many women feel they have no place but subservience in a relationship. *Too often the woman seeks self-worth by having a child even if the circumstances are wrong.* But we are biologically equipped to make all the choices in the relationship game, especially the responsibility of pregnancy.

If you choose a man to have children with, then you'd better be ready to take responsibility for keeping him comfortable *and* raising the children at the same time. Building a family that lasts takes true partnership, which means not just concentrating on the children, but also maintaining the relationship between the parents. All too often partners 'fall asleep' and allow their work and children to take precedence over each other.

*It is our theory that when marriages fall apart it is usually either because the woman needs more romance or the man needs more sex.* Whichever it is, both partners need to be cognizant of each other's needs and women especially have to remember that sex is a major need in a man's life. After all these years together, Paul and I have instituted 'Sunday Sex' as an integral part of our intimate lives. Because 'Hollywood sex' is portrayed as spontaneous, making a weekly appointment sounds unromantic, but once you get started......!

## Serial Monogamy

Some anthropologists and other scientists believe that women are designed to be *serial monogamists*.[48] That is, we look for mates who will be good supporters of our offspring until those offspring become self-reliant enough to survive if necessary. That is surmised

---

[48] David Barash & Judith Lipton, *The Myth of Monogamy*, 2002. Sarah Blaffer Hrdy, *The Woman That Never Evolved*, 1999. Christopher Ryan & Cacilda Jethá, *Sex at Dawn: The prehistoric Origins of Modern Sexuality*, 2010.

to be at about seven years old, an age when the child has the brainpower and enough physical strength to be able to forage for itself, at least in a natural environment. Hence the famous 'seven-year itch' and perhaps the number of marriages that end in divorce at multiples of seven years.

Remember it's your body and your responsibility and that there is no automatic guaranteed safety net. This makes it imperative for women to carefully select their partner and to be prepared to shoulder the burden of child rearing alone if a poor choice is made. I know the biological urge to create life is powerful, but your own life needs to be created wisely first, or everyone involved will be damaged.

## 2: *MEN ARE MORE FEARFUL OF WOMEN THAN WOMEN ARE OF MEN.*

If you don't remember anything else from this book, keep this in mind whenever you meet a new man. Whatever embarrassment or lack of confidence you are feeling in his company, he's feeling them too, and more so. It doesn't seem that way, because men wear the Male Mask, which gives them the appearance of being tough and self-confident in most situations. But being exposed to the full force of feminine power can make them insecure, weak little boys and they need your help and guidance, which of course opens the door for seduction.[49]

### A Level Playing Field

His apparent aloofness and coolness towards you is most likely caused by fear. While he's doing his best to keep his Mask on, he's feverishly searching for something to say that won't trigger a rejection from you, which is his greatest dread at this moment. So remember and believe in your heart that you are on a far more level

---

[49] Bradley Gerstman, Christopher Pizzo, Rich Seldes, *What Men Want*, p13

playing field than you thought you were. This should give you more confidence to make your approach, and confidence is very attractive. Just knowing that the simple act of talking to him is giving him pleasure (even while he's quaking in his boots) gives you a head start. Both of you are getting something out of this simple first approach - he is flattered and pleased that you are talking to him and you are taking the first step in guiding your own life. Even if he's not The One, you're gaining confidence and so is he. How many situations are so win-win?

## 3: *WOMEN ARE THE CHOREOGRAPHERS OF RELATIONSHIP.*

The choreography and seduction start with courtship and continue throughout relationship. You are the best teacher of relationship skills and you are equipped emotionally and physically for guiding a relationship into true partnership. You will teach him how to be intimate and to please you. You are the one who will shape the emotional quality of your partnership. You are the one who will change your partner from the free-roving lone wolf he dreams himself to be into the protector of your nest, where you set the scene and guide your lives together. Your best chance lies with a Beta male who will be more willing to please and learn than an Alpha male. With your continued application of gentle 24/7 seduction, he will soon learn the steps of the dance and will enjoy the lessons!

### The Spell of Your Brilliance

If you want your relationship to last, you need to begin the choreography of seduction right from the start. That includes your first meeting with him, when you can make the evening revolve around him, making him dizzy with attention, or you can let the spotlight fall on the Fabulous You, and make him fall under the spell of your power. Bewitch and beguile and keep him guessing. Don't expect him to know all the steps in the flirtation dance; you are the choreographer. You may have to improvise, but you do have the intuitive skills that will put him under your spell. It will happen naturally because you are both hard-wired to take your positions in the dance. You will lead him without him knowing it and, like all good teachers, make him feel good about his newly learned skills.

## 4: *I AM WILLING TO WORK TO FIND A PARTNER.*

That seems obvious, but we are up against the Fear Factor again. It's easier to do nothing than to do something. But nothing happens if you do nothing, except your secret long, slow dialogue with yourself, eventually leading to perpetual loneliness. Entropy is a law of Nature, but it can be held at bay, if you're Willing To Work. So, you must be willing to put some effort into initiating a relationship in order to transform your loneliness and waiting into a loving partnership.

### It's a Trip

You need to think of the forming of a partnership as an exciting trip, with day-to-day experiences that you may never have again. You're building something and, just like owning a house, the work is really never done. There are always maintenance and remodeling and improvements to make. It's a commitment to creating something that didn't exist before, and with it comes responsibility.

As we know, women are the architects of successful relationships, at least in the beginning, because most men have no idea how to go about it if they've never been in a successful partnership before. All he has to go by is the relationships he has seen before, in real life or in the movies. And, while he may be a great organizer or manager, he doesn't have the innate ability a woman has that helps to create successful life partnerships. It does come naturally for us women to create the nest and the partnership, by helping a man change his destructive habits, by creating the opportunity to communicate openly, by broadening his emotional range and by making him feel safe and **comfortable** with you.

## 5: *I WILL DATE OR CALL MANY MEN IN ORDER TO FIND THE RIGHT ONE.*

This one is a tool for keeping hope alive when a prospect turns out to be a lost cause. Nothing happens overnight and all skills take time to perfect. You need practice to get your dating 'muscles' working and that means you need to find yourself as many prospects as you can and talk to them. Just talk, if that's all you feel like doing. Talking eliminates fear and helps sort out your fantasies from reality. The more you do it the easier it becomes. It doesn't matter if they appear to be prospective Mister Rights, you need to talk to men who may not live up to the ideal picture you have in mind. For one thing, you need to hone your verbal skills and your psyche needs the practice.

Many women give up trying when their Ideal Man doesn't turn up right away. We've said it before and will say it again – Mr. Perfect doesn't come ready-made. Your innate seductive skill is how you guide a man into being the partner you need, and he will be a better man for your guidance. You're looking for the qualities you desire, but they may not be fully developed in him until you show him how much those qualities mean to you.

Start by practicing standing tall, smiling and looking into men's and women's eyes and saying hello. Take note of all the positive responses. People are hungry for some kind of pleasant contact. In a grocery store see what someone has bought and ask if they have a good recipe for it. In our projects, such as the documentary film we are producing, we've found that some of our best contacts have come from chance meetings. A man we met at a local café was wearing an interesting pair of shoes, so we started asking about them, and he turned out to be an experienced film-maker, whose advice and skill was very helpful.

## An Enthralled Stranger

The point to remember is that you're doing this for you, that you're actively going about the business of changing the course of your own life for the better. It's not about being an easy lay or a tease. It's about talking, one human being to another, getting accustomed first to the idea of talking to a stranger, then getting used to being your powerful self in the presence of a stranger - a stranger who is already enthralled by you, simply because you came over to him or made obvious signals that you wanted to talk to him. Your confidence will fascinate and frighten him, like a deer in the headlights.

## Practice Makes Perfect

Practice makes perfect, and the more confidence you have, the easier the conversation flows, the more attractive you become and the more you can concentrate on the finer details of the man. Everyone reacts to the warmth of a personal remark and it's good practice for you to chat to strangers in the daily course of your life. Even Paul, who used to be the reserved Englishman in public, has become used to just making pleasant small talk and joking with anyone he cares to. It brightens his day and brings a smile to others, even in the middle of their workday, when they are usually operating on autopilot.

I've found it so easy to make anyone smile and feel good, just by a simple compliment on his or her appearance or behavior. After all, everyone has **something** you can compliment him or her on and it takes such little effort and gives such pleasure, that it feels good giving it too. And it helps you understand the hidden depths that everyone has. We all have unique lives and interests, and a simple short conversation can reveal so much about the people who normally pass you by.

When you reach the point where you are at ease talking to attractive strangers you can be as selective as you want to be. You will be less taken in by externals, you'll learn not to judge a book by its cover and will know the questions to ask that will reveal what you need to know and keep him at ease at the same time.

## A Thousand Words

A look is worth a thousand words. You see someone attractive across the room. You study him before he sees you. You notice his face, posture, body type, smile, hair and clothes in an instant. Then he turns his head to look around the room and you avert your eyes. When you look back at him, you see he's looking at you, but he averts his eyes. You wait until he looks back at you again and you smile. He smiles too, then turns back to his conversation. What did that mean? The fact that he averted his eyes then looked back at you and smiled means he's interested in you. When he turned back to the conversation he was having, he was already thinking of ways to get across the room to you, and what to say that wouldn't make him look like an idiot.

You give him a couple of minutes to get away from his friend and come over to you, but he doesn't, although he quickly glanced your way while nodding his head and eating another cracker. If he doesn't approach you in the next few minutes, what are you going to do?

In your previous incarnation, you would probably have waited and waited, and possibly been deeply disappointed when he didn't come over to you. It would have reinforced the low self-esteem you had. You 'knew' there was something wrong with you, and you think he could obviously spot it from across the room. You might have moped around for a while, stealing glances at him as you went about your socializing business, and then decided it was time to go home. Another lost opportunity.

## His Paltry Repertoire

Well, that was then. Now you know that he didn't come over to you because, even though he noticed you and was attracted to you, he couldn't think of anything to say that was a dazzling opening line. While he was trying to concentrate on the conversation he was in, he was going through his paltry repertoire of one-liners, palms sweating and stomach sinking as he told himself, "I'm going to sound like a complete jackass and anyway, it's getting late and I have to get up early for work tomorrow and she's probably engaged or something and anyway what could I talk about, and this party's getting boring and maybe I ought to go home and watch the Weather Channel and just my luck there'd be someone I wanted to meet, but she must be in the other room now, obviously not interested in me." And all the other rationalizations he had for not making the effort to talk to you.

Do any of them sound familiar? I bet you've come up with a mental list a mile long of excuses for not talking to someone. So there you both were, making excuses and missing out on whatever might have happened. Perhaps nothing special, but **who knows?** So what's the solution to the situation? Remember your mantra "he's more afraid of me than I am of him", then **go over and talk to him!**

In my experience, some women, especially in their thirties and forties, are kind of self-righteous about needing the man to make the first approach or call, as if it were owed to them for all their suffering at the hands of patriarchy. And they then put men down for not being brave enough to approach them, even though they're emanating this defensive anger, which often shows in their eyes and posture. It's confusing and mystifying for men, and I think it's time to stop the blame. All it takes is to tap into your feminine empathy and to decide to take charge of your own life.

## He Will Be Grateful

The look you gave him started it all, so now you can follow up with a little conversation. And contrary to his and your fears, it doesn't really matter what you say to open it up. The important thing is that you made the effort. It will impress him and perhaps embarrass him a little that you were braver than he was, but mainly he will be flattered that you wanted to talk to him. It's a good start, and you can say whatever you like and he will think it's brilliant. It could be something as banal as complimenting him on his shirt, or as timeworn as asking him if you've met each other before. You could ask him if he'd like to talk, because you're bored. It doesn't matter. If you give him the chance to talk to you, he will be flattered and grateful.

Years ago, when I thought about talking to a man, I immediately invalidated myself, like saying to myself "Nothing I say is interesting to a man" My brain went dead and my body cold. It's amazing what we can do to sabotage ourselves.

## Hanky Panky

If you are still nervous and want to be more subtle, you could simply walk over close to where he's standing. He will be more inspired the closer you are. Keep thinking, "He's more afraid, he's more afraid..." Make it easy for him to make the move, if you don't do it first. Give him a reason for talking to you. The time-honored ploy of dropping something, like a handkerchief, in his vicinity will give him a perfect excuse for talking and feeling like a hero to start with instead of a bumbling idiot.

My mother and I were once in a hotel where we knew no one. I suggested we drop a handkerchief- just as a test. I couldn't believe it, but it worked! We were soon having afternoon tea with a charming man. It may sound corny, but those Victorians knew a thing or two about getting attention, no matter how uptight they may have seemed. If you don't carry a handkerchief (maybe you should think about carrying one, just in case), use something else. You should probably draw the line at the glass of red wine spilled on his white shirt, but then again, all's fair in love and seduction!

## Girls' Night Out

Here's a very important piece of advice that most women don't think about. When women go out, they are often in groups. There is nothing more intimidating to a man than approaching a bunch of women having a good time together.[50] This is just too much like his painful high-school memories. It's difficult enough to approach a woman on her own or with one other woman, more than that is almost certain to put him off. Men know from bitter experience that when women are in groups, the atmosphere changes and they're probably not interested in being approached by men. Sometimes it's a girls' night out, a chance for them to get away from their guys and just have some female fun without any pressure.

So, if you're in a group of women friends and you see a man who's sending meaningful glances your way and you find yourself attracted to him, get away from the women for a while to give him a chance to come over. Better yet, in true *Seduction Redefined* fashion, go over to him, but don't tell your friends what you're going to do, unless you want all eyes to be on you and him.

You could meet him anywhere anytime, so you have to be ready and thinking on your feet. Again, the more practice you have, the easier it will be for you. You could be in an elevator, on a bus, train or airplane, you could be walking down the street or out jogging with your dog, you could be kayaking on a lake, or you could be at home when he comes to repair your stove. Be adaptable and don't give in to that paralyzing fear. A quick trick to alleviate anxiety is breathing deeply all the way into your belly and exhaling all the way out while

---

[50] Bradley Gerstman, Christopher Pizzo, Rich Seldes, *What Men Want*, p. 30

repeating the following mantra: he is more afraid, he is more afraid. Make him **comfortable,** be soft and strong. Redefine Seduction.

### Suggesting a Date

Most urban women under fifty don't talk about 'dating' any more. They talk about hooking up and about going out with someone, but 'date' means something stilted and uncomfortable to them. I think the word itself is still useful, so when I say "date" I want you to think of it as a positive experience – scary perhaps, but not something painful. So, first, don't think about "asking him for a date", think of it as a suggestion that if he is in his right mind he won't pass up this opportunity to spend some time with the delectable you. That's a good start, because, if he says no, it's his loss.

First of all, make plans to meet midweek, if possible. If he's got any social life at all, it's probably busiest at weekends. Or give him plenty of notice, even up to ten days or so, but be specific about the day. Don't just suggest "going out sometime". If you're doing some activity together, pick something that won't take more than a couple of hours. Do not take him to a family celebration, like Thanksgiving, unless they already know him, or you know him well and this is the first time you've thought of him romantically. Otherwise, it will usually be very **uncomfortable** for him, and you want to avoid that at all costs.

So where to? It has to be something you and he can afford, preferably doesn't require buying a whole new wardrobe and that you think you will both enjoy. Open air is good in the right weather; outdoor concerts, ballgames, picnics, amusement parks, carnivals or just taking a walk in the park or on the beach, all these are great places to talk and get to know each other with little pressure. For indoor activities, there are museums, casinos, art openings, book signings, indoor sports like skating or bowling (although if you're really good at the sport be prepared to play down to his level – this is not a competition!), video arcades, monster truck shows, it all depends what interests you.

Dinner at a restaurant is of course a standard option, although there's the bill to consider and who pays it, which is still a source of unease between men and women. Perhaps it's best to ask up front if he's the old school, man-pays-bill type, or if you're up because you suggested this date, or if Dutch is spoken at this table! Be financially prepared for any eventuality, because there are no strict rules; just don't have a tug-of-war with the bill. My suggestion is that wherever you meet, you try not to sit across from each other. Most restaurants will set a table for two with opposing settings, but sitting next to each other or at adjoining sides of a table is much more conducive to comfortable conversation, as well as accidental physical contact. Also, the two of you don't have to maintain eye contact at all times, and when conversation lapses there are always the rest of the diners to look at and talk about!

Bars and clubs can be an option, and alcohol can serve either as a divine gift of warmth, ease and laughter or can be the demon alcohol that evaporates judgment and memory.

Whatever the venue, it's a backdrop for you – somewhere that shows you at your best. But don't get anxious about planning everything perfectly. Life happens, and let's face it, it's really not going to be the end of the world if it doesn't work. You're surrounded by available men. Be brave and flexible and trust in your feminine power.

# CHAPTER SIX

## Paul: Initiating

### *Understanding Men's Insecurity*

*Novelist Margaret Atwood asked women what was their greatest fear concerning men. The most common reply: A man might kill them. When she asked men to confide their greatest fear concerning women, the most common response: A woman might laugh at them.*
Leonard Shlain, *Sex, Time and Power.*

Coming out of a separation after fourteen years of marriage, I was in bad shape, even though I lived in two different paradises in this period – Hawai'i and Northern California. I wallowed in my self-righteous sense of betrayal and tried to evoke as much pity as possible for my pain, which of course was another *display*. There are, after all, some women who like to rescue men in misery and perhaps I might get lucky! If I had even thought about how callous that was, I was so into my passive-aggressive Male Mask that I probably would have said well hey, it would serve every woman right because one of them had hurt me. And it was a great excuse to drink a lot and write bad poetry.

Now I know that I was at least as responsible for the failure of my marriage as my wife was, but at the time it was a huge blow to my vision of masculinity. So I compensated by becoming a ridiculous, pale version of the classic Hemingway figure – tough, drunk and plagued by his muse - all as a way of bolstering my confidence that I was still a Man.

I dined out on stories of storms at sea and exotic ports. I worked at remodels and repairing termite damage on clients' houses (love those termites!). I continued to work off my rent by caretaking the estate I lived on. And I tried to avoid meeting my ex-wife, so that I wouldn't have to face down my faults. In short, I lived the slowly decaying life of a Beta Male wallowing in self-pity, until circumstance and the kindness of neighbors brought me to mainland USA.

My fears were just below the surface. The fear of entering another relationship that didn't work out. The fear of meeting someone attractive, only to be rejected. The fear of having to face my own complicity in the failure of my marriage. The fear of getting into a relationship that made me want to stay in one place, with one woman.

As bad as my mental state was at the time, the idea of my having to learn new ways was frightening, as I think it is for most men. My past life as a yachtie had given me a taste of freedom, as well as a healthy knowledge of my personal insignificance in this big beautiful world. (Being two weeks from the nearest land will do that to you!) And I didn't think I was ready to give up whatever "freedom" I had now.

The scenario I hadn't thought of was of meeting a woman who would be attracted enough to something she saw in me that she would be willing to work at seducing me. I just figured that if I met someone I would have to do the work, and that was not for me any more.

## Fear of Rejection/Fear of Success

Men's attitudes toward initiating contact and relationship are formed early on and help lead to the creation of the Male Mask. Many men's lives are all about projecting image and covering past injuries inflicted in our teen years, the time when girls change shape and gather in tight, giggling groups in the corridor, suddenly strange and inaccessible. Then, as we boys try to understand and catch up to their maturity, we sprout zits and erections without warning, our blood rages and our minds become mush around these objects of a rampant desire over which we seem to have no control.

Every so often, one of us would muster enough nerve to walk up to that girl he had ignored for so many years, but now couldn't seem to keep out of his dreams. Blushingly aware of every burning pustule and stammer, he dredges up enough words from his blank brain to ask her out, only to be met with an incredulous stare and, if he's lucky, a cold smile as she says No. As he makes his way, slump-shouldered and beet-red, back to the rock from under which he crawled, his ears ring to the whispered "OhmyGods" and the laughter behind him. How could it turn out like that? It had all seemed so simple while lying in bed the night before with an erection.

There's the beginning of the damage, the start of the misunderstandings, the beginning of the fear of rejection, of a sense of the vulnerability of our masculinity, the power of women and a major part of the reason for constructing the Male Mask. Even as adults, men are still nervous about making the first approach to a woman. Especially when she's in a group of other women. Remember what we've said before: ***Men are more afraid of women than women are of men.***

There are many good reasons for this, chiefly the fear of rejection that was instilled in us. But there's also the fear of success! What if she swallows that corny pickup line, and says she would like to go out with you. Up comes the creeping fear that she will ensnare you somehow. Once you're involved in any way, there are expectations. Commitment! (What was I thinking? Why didn't I just stay home and watch the ballgame?) Then there's that underlying fear we all have about sex — we crave it so deeply, yet there's always performance anxiety and once you've been to bed with her there are all kinds of new expectations. We shudder even as we are drawn in, like flies to a Venus Flytrap. We have reason to be afraid and we are.

And it doesn't get any easier even after you've done the relationship thing many times. The only reason I was about to get involved with Donna after we'd "fallen to the floor," as she calls it, was because she said, "No strings attached." Now, of course, even if a woman says that, we still feel the fear of commitment. I know I did and, as it turns out, Donna was full of it. There *were* strings, naturally, but it took a year or so to seduce me and by that time I was willing to commit, thanks to Donna's intuitive skills and patience.

Those are the obvious fears, involving rejection or the ordering of our future lives. But at the moment we meet a woman, we experience a fear of the unknown, because, to most men, women are mysterious creatures. And most of that never goes away; women think differently from men and speak a different language. Unless we commit the brain science to memory, no matter how long we are in partnership with a woman, we may still be surprised from time to time by their reactions and responses.

## The Tyranny of Cultural Myth

Most women do not know about our fear of them. It's a startling revelation to most of them. Women don't see our fear, so they expect us to be as cool as can be, as members of the Confident Guy Club, thanks to the Male Mask we're wearing. As soon as a man approaches a woman, the pressure's on to be as confident as he can, or he'll really come across as a dweeb. Women don't know what we're going through, because many of them don't think they're worthy of our attention. They think *they* have a monopoly on the sweaty palms and heart palpitations that happen around attractive strangers.

The irony is that most men don't know that women are generally fearful of rejection as well. So all the while a man is thinking that the woman he has his eye on is just being cool and has no interest in him, she may actually be too scared to do anything that might attract him.

So, while the man was at the far end of the room, rationalizing why he couldn't get up the courage to go over and talk to her, she thought he wasn't attracted to her and was avoiding her (she's thinking it's because her breasts are too small/big, her hair is too curly/straight, he's so cute, why would he want to talk to an ugly girl like her, and so on).

It's ridiculous how difficult men and women have made this, isn't it? Any guy who wasn't taught the truth about women early on has very little idea what they're all about. And in turn, women have a pretty minimal understanding of men, plus they operate in a culture that gives the edge to males over females, which can only lower their self-esteem and warp their view of men in general. But the advantage that women have in taking the risk of rejection is that they have a brain that can sort out their hurt feelings, while men do not have the same access to emotion that women do, they cannot process the feelings as easily and the damage persists.

The strange thing is that, when it comes to finding a partner, we men have learned very well from all the rejections we've experienced that women have the final power to choose. Yet our culture has decreed that women should not act on their choices until they are approached by men, and that has put the load on men. A woman may feel a deep, biological attraction to a man standing right beside her, but doesn't feel comfortable doing anything about it until he does something.

Every man in the room may approach her, but they don't attract her, so she rejects them, yet she feels powerless to talk to the one man in the room to whom she is attracted. And what if he also feels insecure and does nothing? He can't live up to his notion of what a Manly Man would do and she denies her own power by acting down to her cultural perception of femininity. They both go home alone, back to their TV and dog or cat, and kick themselves for having missed out on the opportunity of a lifetime.

That's the tyranny of cultural myth. And I must admit, I've fallen victim to the fear many times. It's a strange thing, because I'm six-four and good-looking in a big, hairy, freckly kind of way, but I have been in situations like the one I just described, and, yes, I've gone home and beaten myself up for not approaching an attractive woman. Other times, I've felt no fear, or was overcome by desperation, and approached a woman and, bingo, I was in luck! Then of course, there are the many times, when I felt sure of myself and got smacked down.

## Strangers On A Train – An Inside View of the Masked Male

Imagine this scene: A commuter train to the city. Everyone is seated. A man is on the aisle next to an empty window seat and three rows down he sees a woman sitting on the aisle facing his way. He is immediately attracted to her. She glances up at him as he is staring at her, so he looks away. After a couple of seconds, he looks back in her direction. She's still looking at him. She smiles. His heart jumps and he smiles a little back at her, then looks down at his newspaper while he tries to think of a good pickup line.

A shadow falls across the front page that he's not really reading. He looks up and she is standing there. She asks if the window seat next to him is taken. He looks at the seat as if someone might suddenly have appeared there without his knowing it, and then says "No," and he makes room for her to slide in past his knees. She moves in sideways, facing him and smiling, and then sits down in a wave of warm fragrance. She starts a friendly and enjoyable conversation with him, which ends as the train pulls into the city, with her asking him what he's doing after work.

How does that scenario feel to you? Should the man feel belittled and emasculated? Or flattered, and glad that he didn't have to go through the whole fear of rejection thing?

And how would you feel about her? She didn't come on too strong, no sexual innuendoes or anything more provocative than putting her hand briefly on his arm as they shared a laugh. Do you think she's a slut, hussy, tramp, trollop, slattern, floozy, flirt, whore, jezebel, vamp, femme fatale and an easy lay? (By the way, isn't it amazing how many synonyms there are for a woman that is sexually active? Couldn't be sour grapes from previous rejections, could it? After all, "Ah, she's just a slut," sounds much more manly than, "Oh, she didn't want to date me.")

Do you think of her in those terms, since she was attracted to him, as he was to her, and she did something about it? Should she still be attractive to the man, or should he be suspicious of any woman who would make the first advance? Should he be scared of her? Should he feel threatened? Should he check for his wallet as he leaves the train?

It's unavoidable for him to feel somehow at risk, since it is a natural thing for men to be on their guard for any threat. But perhaps it's time for men and women alike to let go of the judgmental attitude towards a woman with a sense of her own power. She is a person with the nerve to get up and do what she feels needs to be done, even if it's only to satisfy her curiosity about some guy on a train. I would advise the man to be vigilant as always (after all, we live in a society in which there are human predators of all sorts), but not to be overly suspicious just because a woman made the move he could have made. She doesn't think he's any less of a man for being smart and flexible enough to have a conversation. He may have impressed her with his sparkling wit. So both of them have passed a few minutes pleasantly and there's a possibility of something more. Congratulations to both of them if it continues further!

*Seduction Redefined* asks women not to give in to their misgivings about what a man will think of her if she makes the first move – "If I talk to him will he be threatened/repulsed/angry? Will he think I'm a prostitute or a mugger?" – and it asks men to be grateful and to give her a chance. We all know what arbitrary rejection feels like; but we don't want men to take out their adolescent damage on a strong and courageous woman.

## Keep Your Eyes Peeled

What does *Seduction Redefined* mean for the mythic, all-American Alpha man, supremely skilled at everything, impervious to pain, immune to emotion, strong yet gentle, stern and square-jawed, a godlike, omniscient father figure? Well, probably not much. But for the everyday regular guys, stuck in a rut, hungry for affection, scared of commitment, clueless about fatherhood, less sexually experienced than we like to admit, very horny and maybe a little pudgy, it means that feminine magic can happen anywhere, anytime, to any man. We all have hundreds of potential partners out there and they could be right next to us - wherever we are. We don't want to stop anyone, woman or man, from making the first move. After all, it takes two to make a partnership so, ladies, if some brave chap does make the first move, treat him tenderly, but remember you are the ultimate decision-maker in whether or not to invest time in this person.

# CHAPTER SEVEN

## Donna: Seducing

### *The How-to of Intricate Seduction*

*No seduction can proceed without creating illusion, the sense of a world that is real but separate from reality.*
Robert Greene, *The Art of Seduction.*

This chapter is the meat and potatoes of my seduction of Paul. I will share with you the seduction dance that I continued around him for over a year and a half before HE asked to move in with me. The advice I give here is valuable and realistic for the young and inexperienced as well as the old and rusty. I guarantee you that any male, even a few sexually aggressive Alphas, will love being the object of serious and creative seduction!

I had no expertise in designing my seduction of Paul. It was simply related to my early enculturated romantic fantasies. I gave myself permission to intuitively and spontaneously exercise those illusions, made of candlelight, music and delicious romantic visuals from the movies I grew up with, which fed my sexually driven body. Of course, my personal approach was one of artistic high drama, since that's my style, but the same results can be achieved by more subtle methods, as the following chapters will describe.

With creative glee I became every sexy star rolled in one. Starting with speaking in soft tones and using sexual innuendo, I truly felt my feminine power and stood straight and proud. The best and most amazing part was it wasn't about manipulation or wanting 'forever', it was about pure pleasure and fun. Indeed, I was in the NOW.

I knew he was enjoying me as much as I was enjoying him because I knew that I was making him comfortable with laughter, his favorite foods, good wine, great music and our sexual attraction to each other. Wisely, I did not mention relationship or the future. I felt so confident that self-doubt had little importance during the seduction, except during the days and nights before our next meeting, which caused me a little angst. That was quickly remedied by making a phone call to him, when he would say - "I'll be over, what time?"

## Discovering Poetry

But first I must tell you about discovering poetry as a tool to deflect (cool down) the unbelievable passion I felt for this man! I didn't have enough energy to go all night every night, but what to do with the energy during the in-betweens? I've read a lot of poetry but always considered myself non-verbal - only expressing myself in imagery on canvas and paper. When my motor went on, so did the lights - sparklers - fireworks - and big creative courage.

Paul was still in pain from ending a fourteen-year marriage. My most brilliant intuit was that he did not want to think of the future, let alone hear any words of commitment or love. He is from London, well-educated, well-read and politically aware. I really didn't have an accurate assessment as to how I would match up to his attributes. Would just sex keep him interested in me? I can cook and discuss the news of the day and I soon discovered I could write poetry. As coincidence had it, a dear friend and sister of the poet Linda Gregg gave me a book of her poems. To get started I cheated a bit by a using a couple of her lines but soon after that I found a comfortable, simple style of short lines which seemed close to my sensual heart and 'down there'. Writing the poetry also assuaged the lonely times between our passionate visits. The pleasure of writing became almost as strong as the actual physical seduction, but then, it was an important part of seduction. Oh, the power of romance! Again, I intuitively knew that if he received something sensual everyday, he would be drawn to me, so almost every other day I mailed him a poem.

## Something to remember...

During your Seduction phase it is critical that you understand that most men cannot respond with the same emotional depth as you. For a very long time, my successful mantra has been - HE IS NOT ME AND CANNOT BE ME. Most men's brains simply do not have the anatomy to be as expressive of their inner feelings as women are, unless they've had a very special upbringing. Women's brains are very different from men's in their structure, with four times as many connections between the right and left hemispheres. There is no way they can think, feel or react as we do. Although gay men and transgenders have greater similarities with women in brain structure than straight men do, men cannot truly be women.

You could play hard to get at this stage, but I don't recommend it. This is *Seduction Redefined*, not *The Rules*. What you are doing is letting him feel his freedom and letting him know that he's charming you, not that you're simply leaving everything to him and giving him all the power in the relationship. It is your timetable, but it must be flexible, to give him space to breathe if he needs to. You can begin to make yourself unpredictable, but never lose touch with him or wait for him to call you simply because it's what he's *supposed* to do. You are creating yourself as the object of desire in his mind. If he's too eager and pushy, you can try to hold him at bay – whatever you're comfortable with. But most men are unsure of themselves in a new relationship, so it's up to you to do your biologically-ordained best to build a relationship with the right man.

## Being The Object of Desire

Just as no one is satisfied with their physical appearance, so no one feels their lives are complete. There is always something missing, we think, in our character or our achievements. The Male Mask is a man's cover for his perceived deficiencies as well as being the required cultural masculine front he must put on. Never take a man at face value, because you'll miss the real person under the Mask. You may be able to tell by his off-the-cuff remarks, by his gestures and reactions what he thinks he is lacking. You may spot a romantic under a hard-bitten shell, an unsatisfied adventurer behind the hip exterior, the man who longs for the exotic behind the bland façade.

You can be the fulfillment of his deepest wishes. You must be aware at all times during the seduction of his behavior and little giveaways, which will tell you more about who he really is and who he wants to be than anything he says up front. Concentrate on the details, because the little things that make him tick, that he lacks and likes, are the most valuable information you can know about him. They're the keys to his heart and the windows to his mind.

If you can tell what your man thinks he lacks, you can help him understand that you can provide what he needs, whether that is companionship, a sense of exotic adventure or simply being the center of attention for a while. Everyone has some degree of need for attention and everyone likes to be able to talk about themselves or air their views. Make yourself a willing listener, but without letting the conversation get too one-sided. There's a line between getting attention and domination that you don't want him to cross.

Similarly, don't forget *your* mission and talk too much – keep the balance.

## Amplify Your Feminine

It's time to create and amplify your Feminine. The Feminine is a mystery to most men, but it is their biological target and need. He knows instinctively that partnership is the goal. He doesn't know why and he wouldn't be able to explain it - this isn't a verbal thing. Usually, when pressed, he will explain it, as women do also, in terms of marriage and mortgage.

Your power at this time is in your being simply a woman, with all the mystery that holds for him. The strange mix of mother and whore that men crave makes all women potential partners for him. He probably isn't that choosy when all's said and done, so it's up to you to make the chemicals react between you, if you feel some attraction there already. But he does want what other men want – a woman who is attractive to him and others, a woman who 'resonates', a woman who can offer kindness.

Women are biologically designed to attract men. The Feminine draws them in to **comfort, softness, protecting arms, sex, kindness, empathy and sustenance.**

## Bemuse, Amuse, Attract

The man you desire must be made to feel physically comfortable, fascinated, slightly off-balance psychologically and bewitched by you. That seems like a tall order, but, really, you do have that head start of being of the opposite sex. Just about everything a woman does, when she's following her Feminine, is different from the way men do things. In general, women have different priorities, outlooks and methods, which men find bemusing, amusing and attractive, even when they try to act cool or laugh at you for being the way you are. We are an endless source of fascination for them, and that is to your advantage.

## Play All Your Selves

It's time to start playing your inner self, or imagine your favorite actress playing the character that is you, without making yourself seem false or too over the top. Think of yourself as the fascinating woman you are, as the star of the movie of your love life. Act out all your fantasies. Make the movie enthralling and inspiring, with plot points along the way to keep the action moving. You don't want your audience to walk out before you're done.

Use your best traits and strengthen your weaker qualities. If you're normally pretty predictable in the way you dress and act, once in a while dress or act a little differently, just to keep the story moving. And that goes for any look you normally have, whether it's REI, Vogue, KMart or full Tribal. It's exciting for a man to be surprised now and again. It keeps him from pigeonholing a woman into one category, and he'll want to stick around to find out who you really are. And all the time he's in your company you can work on him some more. Impress with whatever skills you possess.

While in *eros*, I remember doing any number of things I had never done before. Once I invited Paul to an afternoon art opening in a gallery and I simply wore a feel-good-flowing-flowered-rayon dress without anything underneath. It made me feel a little naughty, and I let him know!

Most men like to feel that they're conquering the woman in some way, so IF your man is the assertive hunter Alpha type (and don't try this if he isn't), use your feminine power to entice him with the rewards of relationship, give him several weeks of attention, then, while he's still interested, distance yourself a little. A touch of moodiness, a hint of mystery, going away for a couple of days without telling him where you're going, then calling him when you get back to keep him off balance - all this lends the mystery and elusive quality that will hook a man like this. Again, it's a fine balancing act. If you make yourself too scarce, or if you come off as a tease, without giving him something in return, he may go hunting for someone else.

## Sounds Like Manipulation

You may be thinking, "This sounds like manipulation to me. It all seems dishonest." But what you're doing here is bringing out aspects of **your *own* authentic personality**, perhaps some aspects that you have kept hidden up until now, because you felt they were unseemly.

I believe that everyone has false self-images due to cultural projections of what the perfect child, daughter, young lady, wife and mother 'should' be. In the same way that men create the Mask, women are often taught to be inauthentic.

*Seduction is the time when you get to discover your real self or selves.*

You are not being a phony as much as you are being all the 'you's' that are inside. This is a new freedom for many of us and makes seduction exciting for both people involved. He is seeing you at your most seductive and you are seeing yourself as someone who is free to seduce and as someone who *knows* how to seduce. When you see the results of that, you begin to feel your biological power and capacity to give and receive pleasure. When you feel that, you begin to get an idea of your potential as a person.

Whether he's the assertive type or not, he is susceptible to your Feminine power. But don't forget that dating is frightening, so invite him to your place for dinner and turn the occasion into a piece of performance art. That's what candlelight dinners are; they create a mood and set the stage for the performance you are about to give. If you have already had sex with him, or believe it's time, think about going beyond the regular candlelight dinner for two. This takes a little courage on your part and some extra thought and preparation, but have fun with it yourself.

Create some theater by setting the scene a little more exotically than he might expect. Dramatic lighting, or hanging fabrics, or exotic or romantic music can lend a tone to an evening that will make it different from any other. Put a poem at his place setting. Or serve dinner on the floor, with cushions to sit on and dim lighting. Prepare finger food that you can feed each other. Or wear a mask and have him wear one, too. Or order exotic take-out food if you don't feel like cooking. If you're at the right stage in the relationship, eat pasta together in the bathtub with your fingers (one of my favorites!), or have a theme for the evening – 50's music and burgers, or Greek music and food, Indian food and a sari.......and, and, and....

*Remember there are two neural pathways to pleasure in every human body – food and sex.*

## Unsettle Him

But if you think the exotic will be too scary for him (or you), do something a little subtler. The goal is to unsettle him slightly, to shake him a little. Next time you date, act differently; if you were coming on strong last time, be more demure; if you were quiet last time, take him dancing and show yourself off. As time goes on, balance returns, but this is the crucial time, when he is looking for excuses to leave and reasons to stay. Give him the reasons that make him fascinated in what comes next.

Dinner and a movie every time you date may be fine, but it's not fascinating. He's more interested in what the movie is like than what you are like. Keep him looking at you and for you, all the while you're giving him attention. Everything you're doing is for his amusement and comfort - at least that's what you want him to think.

Stay in the Now, but invest in the future. You've had dates before, but now you're looking for something more. If you can change your life by being with this man, it's worth a little theater. Plus, it's fun!

Be creative, do things you've never done before but have dreamed of doing. Create a stage on which he can do things you've always wanted the men in your life to do. You will feel good, and so will he, because, if you do it properly, he'll think he came up with the whole scenario.

## Everyone Has Their Thing

Be part of what he enjoys doing. If you're fascinated by what fascinates him, he will feel complimented and safe. Again, don't overdo it. He might see through your over-enthusiastic response to watching the Weather Channel all day or learning the different classifications of railroad cars. Everyone has their thing and, if you're serious about getting together with this man, you must give his thing a chance, just as you expect him to do what you want to do sometimes.

If you do want to build a relationship with him, but can't see yourself going to wrestling matches every weekend, you have the perfect way to keep him from feeling too trapped in a relationship. When the relationship is far enough along, you support his doing his thing often enough that he feels free and manly, while you do your thing at the same time. At some point, if you've done the groundwork, he will miss you while he's at his archeological dig without you and will prefer to spend the time with you.

When Paul invited friends from out of town for a local weekend and didn't invite me, I made plans to be at another weekend event to "forget him". It worked and my trip turned out to be far more interesting than his!

## Together Alone

Most people living alone have made their world sufficient for themselves, which fear and laziness discourage them from changing. Their comfort level seems right, so why make changes? It's up to you to make his world seem insufficient.

If he's a quiet Beta type that only really comes out of his shell in social situations, let him talk about himself when he's with you. He will begin to shine and feel better about himself and he will associate you with those good feelings. As time goes on, you will be able to assert yourself more in the relationship, because he will know you are the source of the higher self-esteem he has been experiencing and will want more and more.

When you reach that stage, it's time to begin to wean him off getting most of his attention from others and to get him to rely more on you than them for social satisfaction. Gradually change his habit patterns and social life so that you and he are alone more often than you are with other people. You will slowly become sufficient for each other, with social occasions being the icing on the cake, rather than the norm.

If you've always gone to the same place on dates and played pool with his friends, it's time to try something different on some of those regular pool nights. Don't cut him off from his friends, just make them a little less important to him than you are. Include yourself in his circle and include him in yours.

Again, does this sound like total manipulation and nothing to do with who you are? Well, if you are serious about forming a partnership with this man, you must understand that anything he does that takes his mind off you is competing with you for his attention. But I'll remind you that I'm not saying you should cut him off completely from anything he likes. The things he likes to do and the people he likes to be around are part of who he is and therefore part of what originally attracted you to him.

His preferences and yours will change naturally as the relationship deepens and life becomes about the two of you together, rather than two people alone. Both of you are going to go through changes that transform you from singles to a couple.

Most of what you're reading here is the natural course of events in a developing relationship. As your feelings for each other deepen, it's only natural for both of you to want to be with each other more often. Your friends and family will naturally become less important to you than the person you might be spending the rest of your life with, or who may be helping you raise a child. The only difference is that we're reminding you to be conscious of this progression and to guide it purposely if you think it is losing its impetus.

If you've been in a long-term relationship before, you probably know what I mean and you're smiling knowingly and feel a mix of pity and hope for our women readers that are doing this for the first time. But this book is about forming not just a relationship, but a **partnership**. That is a situation that all too few women have experienced. It is work and pleasure all in one, something like raising a child.

Children need to be taught and guided and, yes, manipulated, into positive behavior to prepare them for life ahead. So it is with the men in your life. They need to be guided in how to act in a relationship, especially if they've never been in one before. As an artist, I like to think of a man as a beautiful piece of chocolate which women, using their warmth, can slowly shape to the needs of the partnership. You are unique, so no man comes ready-made for you. Sculpt away, oh beautiful one!

### Time Alone

Act subtly to bring the two of you closer together more often. Go with him to his bowling night, but also have him come with you to your regular social events. Most of all, spend time alone with him. This is a romance you're involved in and you two are the main characters in your story right now. Everyone else is a distraction. You are forming a world that includes both of you *and* all your experiences and friends. In time, that world will naturally shed some of the excess baggage of your former lives. No telling what that may be.

Another big reminder: do not make disparaging remarks about the people he's known longer than you. He will remember the comments you make and if he ever needs an excuse to distance himself from you, there they will be in his memory, and they will sound like betrayal. It's certainly out of place until you and he know each other way better.

## Do the Little Things

Keep doing the little things that make him feel good around you. You can write poetry and be flamboyant, but the quiet moments alone, or your hand resting on his arm or shoulder while you're out together are reassuring and endearing. You're creating trust, physical comfort and familiarity with you. Notice what he likes and buy him something he'll use or that he needs. It doesn't have to be expensive, just a little something - a tie, a pen, a baseball cap, his favorite sweet or savory treat - that will remind him of you. It could even be the roll of duct tape he forgot to buy, or something else on his shopping list. You are becoming a part of his everyday life and making him miss you when you're not there.

Do things that will remind him of you, too. If you are in a cafe with paper napkins, put lipstick on and kiss his napkin and put it in his pocket. If you wear perfume and he likes it, put a little on his clothing when he's not looking, just enough so that he can smell you even when you're not there. You're casting a bewitching spell that will make you seem to be a constant in his life. Imagine him having spent the night with you and finding a little memento of you in his jacket pocket at work next day. A pair of panties could be daring and funny, but a love note, a candy, a dried apricot, a cookie could also remind him of you, or a CD of your favorite songs that he finds in his car.

## Do the Taboo

Take him a little way into the realm of the taboo. Do things that "simply aren't done" by regular folks. Give his life a touch of the risqué. You could make him think that you could get a little out of control from the force of your desire for him. If you're both in *eros*, that won't be too far from the truth anyway. Everyone is tempted by the wild side, it's exciting and dangerous and so far from most people's lives that just a hint of it will draw him.

Make your lives a secret, special world. Keep writing to him - little notes and poems at dinner, on his pillow, on the bathroom mirror, in his pocket, in the mail. Send him letters and packages, e-mails and phone messages. You and he will become separate from everyone else, a world unto yourselves, full of secret promise. He will never know when the next reminder of you will appear, which will keep him in suspense and titillated. That's your job, your responsibility, your biological power.

He may not reciprocate these gifts. The movies may tell us that a man will send two-dozen long-stemmed red roses every day, but don't count on it. Early on, I decided it made no difference to me, because my fulfillment was in the giving, not the taking.

## Support Him

As you change his familiar life, he will look to you more and more for comfort and pleasure. You will start to look to him for emotional support and especially declarations of his commitment to you. It's a tricky time for both of you, and the timing has to be right. If he still feels trapped when he thinks about long-term commitment, you must reassure him that you have no intention of trapping him in anything. **Every decision made for the long-term must be made by the two of you as a partnership.**

Make it obvious to him what he would be missing if he chickened out now. If you've done the work, the life he's thinking about returning to will seem less inviting and comfortable without you in it. You are part of his life now, and only you can give him the pleasure that he lacked in his life. Become partners, share everything, keeping your own world intact as you move around in the outside world. You will be his haven and he will be your protector.

## Build the Partnership

Once you have established the feeling of being two people alone in your own world within the world at large, with you as the provider of comfort, pleasure and distraction, it is time to begin to build the partnership you desire. There is no timetable for this, it could happen within weeks or months and the process never ends, because life doesn't end until you leave!

Life brings changes to us all, even those who think they've got their lives all figured out. At the beginning, all is possible, because you and he are the only two people in love in the world and together you can achieve anything. If you want him to take a stronger role in the partnership, back off a little and let him make some of the decisions that you have made up to now.

The whole reason for *Seduction Redefined* is to build partnerships, so you must begin playing equal roles, using your complementary strengths, to make it all work. Two separate people working together to make their lives more complete. You asking him to water the garden if you're not home, or him calling from the grocery store to ask what you need for dinner.

Partnership depends on the intimate bonds that are formed and maintained between partners. Seduction cannot end with the passing of *eros*, but must continue into its *agape* form to sustain the closeness, the spontaneity and the subdued excitement of long-term togetherness. Marriages that become stale breed disharmony and people drift apart. Remain conscious of the feminine power to guide your partner, both at home and in his work, through the most effective means of all – seduction 24/7.

# CHAPTER EIGHT

## Paul: Being Seduced

*Seduction from a Male Perspective*

*There is a difference between [a man's] knee-jerk response to a cute babe and the open-hearted awe and mindless swoon he feels in the company of a woman who moves, breathes, smiles and shines radiant energy like a goddess.*
David Deida[51]


I wasn't the easiest subject for Donna's seduction. I'd had a pretty active sex life in my twenties, when I had been a bluewater sailor. These were my hi-test years, lots of swashbuckling and "manly" doings of all kinds, so it was natural to be "on the prowl" when I reached port. In most instances I would have said at the time that I was the initiator with the women I met, although, thinking back, I can think of at least a couple of times when women approached me.

---

[51] *The Way of the Superior Man*. Deida's guide for living a masculine life of integrity, spirituality and authenticity in love.

I know that I was aware of the signals being transmitted by women, so perhaps the come-ons were more mutual than I thought at the time.

I always tended to be a serial monogamist, meeting and staying with one lover for however long I was in port, so I was always looking for as long a relationship as I could have with these wonderful women, before I left on the next leg of my adventure. Very rarely were there any one-nighters.

When it was time to weigh anchor I would honestly be very sad to leave, but I had that great male excuse that I had a duty to my ship. It's the male dream, finding a caring sex partner who knows that you have some kind of obligation that will take you away soon. No commitment, no promises that can't be kept. I would write to them for a while, but even that obligation would fade, no doubt with a sigh of relief on their part as they went on with their lives and forgot about me. I'm sure they would have appreciated a better lover, and looking back, I know how under-educated I was!

At a party in Guam, my shipmates and I were entertaining some of the resident American women – airline crew and a few of their friends who lived full-time on the island. We were really trolling, as men at sea will do. One of the women caught my eye, so I brought my chair over to where she sat. We were both barefoot, and she noticed now big my feet were. I have almost prehensile toes, so I reached over and took her foot in a toe-grip that had often helped me retrieve items dropped in the bilges.

That simple contact started a chain reaction of passion that lasted until I left the island, then continued when she followed me to another Micronesian island, where she had friends and where our boat was anchored and I would spend the night whenever I could get a ride up the lagoon to where she was. Finally, I left that boat in Bali and flew back to Guam, from where we left to take a journey together that turned into love and marriage, and continued until it ended in a blink of my blind eye, fourteen years later.

That whole process of meeting and falling in love seems to me now to have been a mutual seduction. She followed me and I returned to her. Later, she changed her life for me, sailing the world for several years, then I changed my life for her, and we settled down in Hawai'i so that she could pursue her graphic design career.

I believe I wasn't ordinarily the subject of seduction, beyond some eye contact and signs that I was welcome to approach. But Donna's seductive techniques were completely intuitive, creative and passionately original. I had and have never met anyone like her for pure power of spirit, determination and focus on her goal. And I was that goal!

I never knew what was going to happen next, what her next idea would be. That made me uneasy at times, but I have to say that, despite the feeling I sometimes had of being drawn into a web, it was blinding, deafening and exciting all at once. I was in an almost constant state of sexual arousal – every day felt as if it was my first day ashore after a long voyage.

Donna somehow knew just the right mix of raw pleasure and nurture to make me comfortable. We would eat a gourmet dinner together, then plunge into each other with an intensity that I had never experienced before. She made me feel like a king while I was being seduced. I had forgotten what it was like to feel needed and have my needs met at the same time.

I had to face the fact that I was not in charge of this process and that I was being led into something that might be beyond my control, but, boy, was I having a good time! This was exotic and erotic, I was being tempted with the most delicious food and wine, receiving attention and comfort, and learning things about making love that I wished I'd known thirty years before. Donna was, as she says, "in heat", but she was always aware enough to let me know what she needed in bed (or on the table or the floor....).

It was the most sensual time of my life, mainly because I allowed myself to be the *receptor*, not to try to be the Great Lover, and to accept Donna's role in initiating our partnership. She was and is both teacher and student, lover and nurturer, siren and voice of reason. At the height of the seduction, she would send or hand me an envelope at least twice a week, with a poem full of the most erotic imagery. The barrage of sensuous stimulation kept me on the edge all time. Donna kept up the pressure against all my uncertainty and in the end I surrendered willingly to her.

Donna knew what she wanted and saw in me someone that I didn't even suspect was there. Her use of her biological and intuitive skills turned a wild ride into a lasting voyage, which I would never have had the courage to attempt without her navigational ability. If I'd been in charge of our relationship, it would have been just another great sexual escapade, followed by my jumping ship at the next port of call. But she had changed my way of looking at the world. She had begun the process of turning me into her **partner**.

## A Word to the Wise to Women

During your Seduction of the man you've selected, you must constantly remember to look behind his Male Mask and to be aware of how he is very differently wired and programmed. Remember that while that guy in the cubicle across the office may look calm and in control, and the President of the United States may seem all-powerful and in command, all you are seeing are their Male Masks — the manifestation of a slew of unconscious instructions embedded in their psyches. These instructions are common to most men.

I gave you the Male Mask List from the guy's point of view earlier, but here it is in a slightly more civilized version. Remember, this is the guide for men to be what male-dominated culture calls "Real

Men". It is a combination of the innate and the acquired, of biology and learned behavior.

## "THE MALE MASK LIST"

- **Don't show emotions** — *Talking about love, saying "I love you," talking about being happy or afraid is wimpy. Anger, pride and envy are good motivating emotions. Save other emotions for watching football.* Everyone, even his mother, drums that into a boy through example and instruction. Being manly is all about competitiveness, aggression, stoicism and hiding the emotions. Men are taught to show their caring by their deeds not their words. When he put your bookshelf together, or tightened the fan belt on your car, or drove you to the mall, or did the dishes, or opened the mayonnaise jar for you, it was an act of love.

- **Don't show weakness** — *Not only is it "unmanly," it invites bullying.* This is a lesson learned in school, which boys learn quickly. As all the boys around him are taught to be tough, competitive and to express themselves physically, the playground becomes a battleground where every boy must prove himself. Being male is all about hierarchies of various kinds. It works for boys and men this way; they find their place in whatever situation they are in and operate from that position. Running away is not an option, nor is reasoning. When a boy comes under physical attack, he must stand his ground and fight back. It's primitive and brutal, and it's testosterone doing its work.

- **Be independent** — *Asking for help is a sign of weakness.* The classic example is a man driving in a strange place. He'll stop at a gas station and instead of asking for directions, he'll buy a map of the town, even if this is a once-in-a-lifetime visit. He'll make excuses about the inaccuracies of people's directions, but the truth is a real man cannot show himself to be lacking in knowledge or dependent on strangers. "Real men" can do everything and know everything. That's the external attitude anyway. Inside, they are fearful of new things, places and people, *especially women,* because they pose threats to the male aura of control and that makes a man unsure of his place in the pecking order.

- **Don't admit to needing love or relationship** — *Mom wants to hear it and that's unavoidable, otherwise it's only acceptable when it's demanded.* Men want to *be* intimate, not *discuss* intimacy. Men do need love, but they don't want to talk about it. It's a sign of loss of control and another symptom of dependency to talk about such things, and men must always appear to be in control. If a man starts talking about needing your love or getting serious in your relationship, take notice. This is a huge step for him.

- **Don't let a woman tie you down** — *Commitment leads to complications that take away a man's freedom.* This biological imperative never really goes away, especially with the cultural realities such as paying off mortgages and raising children. All changes that affect his self-image as the independent hero, striding across the world, free and unfettered, should arise from his own decisions. Especially in the early stages, he should feel that he is the one who decided to spend the weekend with you rather than going to the Monster Truck Meet with his buddies. You need to be very careful not to make your man feel as if he's being backed into a corner, or forced to surrender any of his free-roaming ways. *Make him comfortable.*

- **Don't show pain** — *It is unacceptable to admit to pain, especially emotional pain. A true man grits his teeth and acts as if nothing can hurt him.* Hollywood action films have given men a powerful fantasy role model to emulate. The rugged hero, blazing his way through enemy lines, endlessly resourceful, skilled and strong, emerging from hand-to-hand combat unscathed but for a touch of perspiration on his brow and a scratch on his cheek. Impossible to live up to, yet so appealing to the high-testosterone male self-image, these movies have changed male behavior, boosted military recruitment and made the sensitive and evolved man an object of derision.

## What Do Men Really Need?

During the seduction phase a man does need more than easily available sex and good food. Because the Male Mask works so well for men as protection against exterior threats then you will need to make it safe for him to step out from behind it. I believe that there is great relief for men in being able to find someone with whom they can really be themselves. It may even be part of the satisfaction of having kids. A man can finally be himself around his own offspring, at least until they're at an age when the father becomes the disciplinary figure. Then the Mask might go back on and only his wife will know the true him.

There are three needs men have in order to feel comfortable in a relationship.

### 1: *MEN NEED TO HAVE A SAFE PLACE TO EXPRESS EMOTIONS.*

I know, this doesn't sound like a guy thing, but despite all we've been taught about not having to express emotions, we're still humans with a brain that produces emotional responses to everything that happens to us. Psychologists say that the X chromosome we get from our mothers gives us our emotional and social qualities, so they're in there, waiting to be expressed. We just don't have the freeway access to our emotions that women have. But just because a man might not express his emotions, except at a ballgame, doesn't mean they're not stacking up inside him. That can't go on forever without some sort of explosion. If a man is welcomed into a true partnership, he will be able to relax the Mask and actually express how he feels about life and any problems he may have.

### Poker Face

This male need to be able to safely let their guard down is usually a big surprise to women. It's a given that women need to be able to express their emotions, but they usually cannot see beyond the Mask to understand that men have the same need. Bravado, bluff, arrogance, defensiveness and often silence are some of the ways we deal with uncertainty. That's why poker is such a great guy's game, but the poker face of the Male Mask is a barrier to getting the closeness that men crave, even while they're scared of it. Who said men weren't complex? Yes, men are scared of the very thing they *need* from a partner. And that all has to do with the next need - the freedom to roam the great outdoors of our imaginary perfect world.

## 2: *A MAN NEEDS THE SPACE AND THE RECOGNITION OF BEING A MAN IN HIS OWN RIGHT.*

This is about giving a man space to feel that he's not being encumbered. Every man yearns at heart to roam free, even if all we do is sit at home in front of the TV. We all have the need to feel as if we can leave at a moment's notice, as impractical as that may be. It's unrealistic for most of us, in fact it may not even occur to us that we yearn for the open road or anything like it, but in the early stages of a relationship, when the woman starts making nesting noises, most men will feel a chill down their spine and start looking for the exit.

### Fantasy Men

You already know that we have a fear of being tied down; it's a major part of the male myth we cherish so much. "Nobody can tell us what to do, where to go – we're men, damn it, and no-one can regulate our lives!" Well, of course, this is all fantasy, but it's deeply ingrained in our psyches, thanks to our culture. So men need the space to feel like their fantasy image, even while we're being guided into being committed to a stable relationship.

### Time To Go?

That's part of the reason that my very smart partner, Donna, asks me at least once a month on general principle, as well as after a disagreement, "Do you want to leave me now?" For the couple of milliseconds that I think about an answer, I feel as if it's my decision to stay in the relationship. It's a fine line to tread, as with most aspects of partnership. This 'contract' of the freedom to leave is supported by our belief that partnership, even more so than marriage, should be based on trust. We have no legal boxes around our partnership, but we do have many ongoing rituals, with Sunday Sex being the most mutually beneficial!

### 3: *WE NEED FAITHFULNESS.*

This is important to both women and men. How many crimes of passion have occurred because a man thought he was being cheated on? It's a challenge to our masculinity, which is much more fragile than most women know. It's the fear and humiliation of being a cuckold, of being 'less than' a man, of losing face and losing control of our 'possessions'. We think it's the main reason why men created religion and holy matrimony in the first place – to make sure that the genes being passed on to the next generation are his own.

There were no children involved in my case, but when my ex-wife broke the news of her infidelity, I felt betrayed. I was also pompously self-righteous, full of blame and ostentatiously sad. Part of that was from my bruised Male ego, part from the nagging feeling that I had been remiss, unconscious and blind to the signals, part from humiliation as a lover. Since men are so naturally invested in the sexual aspect of love, any aspersions cast on their prowess as lovers is a strike at their emotional core.

Looking back, I can see where my failings in the partnership contributed to our problems, but at the time I was the 'wronged party'. I would never have thought of cheating on my wife, so when her secrets came out I was able to take the moral high ground and make the most of it, sucking up all the sympathy I could get. Pretty embarrassing to look back on it now.

Women whose husbands are having affairs are not 'less than feminine' in the same way that cheated-on men are 'less than masculine'. Perhaps they don't have the same feeling of their Gender - with a capital G - being at stake. What's more important is their trust in their partner and the cultural contract that holds them together.

But faithfulness isn't just about not messing around; it's about a woman being sensitive to a man's self-image, seeing his best side, not embarrassing him in public by exposing his faults to strangers. And also not revealing to anyone but trusted friends what lies beneath his Male Mask that he has spent all his life constructing.

A woman who has seen behind the Mask holds that knowledge in trust, and that's another reason that a man feels his fragile masculinity to be at risk in a relationship. It goes without saying that women also value the intimate secrets they have shared with a partner, but they need to be aware that men are perhaps even more sensitive than women when it comes to self-image.

We men know our fragility even if we don't admit it. We know the world to be a dangerous, even scary, place in which we must seem to be invulnerable. We know that women are the agents of change in our lives, and we fear "emasculation", the dropping of the Mask and the constrictions of family life, at least until we are seduced into it. The innate skill of seduction is the process that gently takes that fear away and helps a man become the fully mindful man he was destined to be.

# CHAPTER NINE

## Donna & Paul: Seduction Hazards

*Overcoming His Fight or Flight Mode*

*The failure to realize that even the most seemingly successful men are, deep inside, unsure of themselves has led women with the best of intentions into difficulties that they have not understood.*
George Weinberg[52]

We all can understand the commitment of a 'real job' - five days a week. Even now it's hard to believe I spent 24/7 seducing Paul and why? Because there was more pleasure than pain for me. But what about him?

After about four months and deep into our passionate meetings, I made a major mistake. I said with a tone of desperation, "When will I see you again?" Lost in my own sensual world, I had forgotten that he had to work all day after all night sex, he was tired and he was

---

[52] *Why Men Won't Commit*, p11

still feeling the pangs of divorce. His fatigue triggered anger and all kinds of ridiculous reasons why he wasn't ready for a 'relationship'. Two days later I received a beautiful 'Dear Donna' letter explaining the many reasons he was the wrong guy for me. I was awake enough to realize my mistake and didn't take it too seriously. Here is his letter almost word for word with my counter response to his each sentence and paragraph:

Paul: Dear Donna, The very thing I feared from the first has come about. There's no such thing as a sexual friendship, or fun without commitment. I've told you right from the start that I'm not ready for the kind of relationship where I have to worry about your feelings of rejection.

Donna: You don't understand that my greatest pain is wanting to know when I will see you next. The game of NOW we are playing is not working for me anymore because I need a commitment of scheduling only. We both have a lot going on and it is difficult to plan. I think just a technical adjustment would cure the problem for me by planning at least our next meeting.

Paul: You think of me as your muse and as a great lover.

Donna: Maybe I shall use the word you used, kindred spirit or like-minded or soul mate - forget muse. You ARE a great lover!

Paul: I can only put this down to the fact that you've opened yourself completely, mentally and physically, to the situation that YOU created.

Donna: Yes, I agree. Remember my Mission Statement: "I shall find a sensual male lover who will laugh, sing and dance". No mention of relationship or commitment. How could any of this happen unless our juices were flowing? I have just come out of a long relationship too. Now I want the fire! Remember when I said "no strings attached"? I thought I made it clear when I said I wasn't ready for another relationship right now ...maybe later. I want it ALL in due time.

Paul: I'm not the inspiration for your poetry and energy. The inspiration comes from your laying yourself bare to new experience, with all the freedom and excitement that so doing can bring.

Donna: Yes, I had done my homework but the bonus of our 'fitting' and your 'little things' have moved me the most.

Paul: But, of course, that's now not enough. Now you've decided you want all the benefits of exploration but from a STABLE relationship.

Donna: Wrong! I have looked realistically at a STABLE RELATIONSHIP or commitment with you and this state of knowing each other - THERE IS NO BASIS FOR ONE. You don't know me. Thus far, we have been in an erotic-seduction four-month loop. When I try to imagine any kind of life with you right now - I don't get a picture. Why, we haven't even been to a meeting together or with friends... so what is this commitment business? Is this a giant projection on me from your past? I think you have translated my physical and emotional passion and lack of scheduling into wanting commitment.

Paul: I don't feel the longing, yearning and desperate need that mirrors the love you have shown.

Donna: Love is a complicated word - Love means investment of time and experience. If you can be in the present with me, what more could I ask? I would hope your word desperate would translate into PASSIONATE. I know my hormones have gone wild. I love it. This is a superb and sublime time for me and before this upset, YOU didn't seem to be suffering.

Paul: The one thing I dreaded from the first was tearful entreaties, name-calling and the heart-shredding need for more love.

Donna: I had no idea I would have such fun with you - joyful sex, intellectual creativity. Can't I adore you? Thus far I respect you and learn so much from you and I love the way you embrace the world around you.

Paul: There is a certain barrenness of emotion on my side that will never allow me to enter wholeheartedly into a relationship. That's the yawning gulf between us - you a sensitive, caring, love-filled seeker of truth and romance, me the once-caring, scarred and scared husk of my former self. Thinking about it now, it looks like a long and lonely track winding over cold hills.

Donna: You sound hopeless but I don't believe you. Your persona expresses another enlightened view - timing is everything. We are all alone and we are all connected.

Paul: So what's the solution? I NEED friendship, laughter, a welcoming embrace and help in seeing the joys of life.

Donna: You've got it babe! I TAKE RESPONSIBILITY FOR MY FEELINGS. My eyes are wide open. I am the one writing the book. Your place or mine on Tuesday?

### Back to The Now

He called after receiving my letter. Then officially I began a conscious effort to keep my seduction of him in The Now. I made each encounter memorable. Thus continued my stage for altering his consciousness and his four senses with sensual music, light and flavors.

He gave me a jump-start by giving me a taped compilation of his favorite music. I played the tape, which helped make him comfortable right at first. Subtly, I found out what his favorite English and American foods were and every now and then I would surprise him with a 'delicacy' – bangers'n'mash, toad-in-the-hole, pizza...

The kitchen was well lit but all the nooks and crannies of the rest of the studio were bathed in candlelight. Dinner moved from the table to sometimes on the floor in front of the fire, to the garden or to our very favorite - the outdoor five-foot sunken bathtub that was conveniently plumbed with hot water. Ahh, sitting in warm water under the trees and nibbling on snack food was pure pleasure. Our laughter and shared stories about ourselves were literally fed with sensual finger food. The one we liked the best was feeding each other pasta, with our fingers of course. All these years later, we can still laugh, sing and dance!

## Where's He Going?

*Seduction Redefined* really means redefining the role women play in initiating and forming relationship, being assertive while retaining sensual femininity. There may be a time in the crucial early stages of dating when the man will start to back away from the budding relationship, and it's then that you will need some of your most powerful seductive techniques, if you still feel that he's right for you.

Perhaps he's not answering the phone, he left on a trip, or he's just withdrawn into his cave without a word. Why? You're going to wonder what you did wrong. Well, there's the possibility that he feels guilty about something, that he lied to you about his being single, that he's sociophobic or a closeted gay, or that he only wanted you for sex and/or company, or perhaps he was only in town for a convention, or he's dead.

These are some worst-case scenarios, of course. Perhaps he just seems distant somehow, not as lively and affectionate to you. Be sure to remain objective about what's happening; don't read too much into his behavior, because at this stage you're likely to be sensitive to minute changes in his behavior. His withdrawal is more than likely caused by his natural, biological fear of entrapment. He least of all will understand why, so it is your female responsibility to coax (seduce) him back to being comfortable with you. This is when you turn on your sex appeal and candlelight - more seduction. That's what I did with Paul, and it worked.

It's a good skill for a seductress to be aware of nuances and ready to pre-empt any negative developments, but you should also be aware that, as a woman, you're biologically biased towards skepticism about the depth of his commitment. According to research by psychologists Martie Haselton and David M. Buss, this skepticism is normal and is a cushion against "falling victim to deceptive signals of commitment intent".[53] Examine the circumstances; is he tiring of you or just tired from overwork? Check your expectations and try to assess whether you're anticipating too much from him at this stage.

## Not NOW

It's quite likely that you scared him off by not staying in the NOW. That is very important at this stage. Even if you can't keep yourself from dreaming about that little house you and he are going to set up together, or the tropical vacations you're going to take together, you must prevent yourself from letting any of your plans seep into what you say. If you start talking about plans that go further into the future than, say, a week, you're lighting up alarms in his brain.

He will go into fight-or-flight mode to save himself from being captured. He is a delicate creature, sensitive, even, in this situation. Think of him as a skittish horse, a feather on your finger, a cornered cat. Your voice must be soothing, with no hint of entrapment or punishment for what you are doing together. If you've been to bed together, he may be having pangs of guilt, because he still doesn't love you as deeply as you might appear to love him. You have to

---

[53] Haselton, Martie G. & Buss, David M., *Error Management Theory: a new perspective on biases in cross-sex mind reading*; Journal of Personality and Social Psychology, January 2000, vol. 78, no. 1, 81-91.

come to terms with that one. Most men will not feel the instant commitment most women feel once they have had sex. It's just the way it is - no blame on that one.

It could be that he got a sense that he didn't want to go out with you again, but didn't know how to say it without hurting you. Or it could be he thinks you don't want to see him again, or that he'd annoy you by phoning you. You know him better than I do - how was his self-esteem? Did he seem to take self-deprecation just a bit too far? Or did he act confident? Was he pushy and brash or quiet and sensitive to your feelings? Did you share confidences? Did anything happen to embarrass either of you? These are all factors to be considered. None of them precludes a call from you.

## Sexual Attitude

*A friend, who describes himself as a Boy Scout compared with most men, says that* **some** *men are programmed not to make love without some kind of commitment. He also says that he and his second wife should have remained just lovers, but he wasn't wired that way. His voices told him he had to be in a committed relationship if he was going to be having sex with her. The sex was wonderful, but marriage didn't work for them.* John Scherer[54]

For most women, the act of sex is a statement of commitment and intimacy that is felt on an emotional, biological and physical level. For most men, it's mostly physical, a rush of endorphins, especially in the early stages of *eros*. With time, sex may become a biological and emotional attachment with someone he feels something for. It's just possible, if you've had sex early in your relationship, that he feels he's taking advantage of you. He may be guilty about it and guilt is a powerful incentive to leave. If he leaves before he gets any deeper into the relationship, he won't have to prolong the self-

---

[54] John Scherer is the author of *Five Questions That Change Everything*, and co-director of Scherer Leadership International. www.scherercenter.com

blame. It may be as simple and clean as that. Men are better at cutting emotional ties than women, because for most men those ties don't go as deep as they do for women, at least early on.

Another reason he may have disappeared is that he was the one who was beginning to feel love over and above *eros*, while you were being hot and heavy into sexual good times. He may be scared of your rejection of him if he appears too serious, or he may have got the wrong impression of you. When you're together, you can talk about the things you like about each other, without getting into talking about love or relationship. As you talk, you may be surprised by how differently you each view your relationship. Don't be offended, because this is just the beginning of the differences in perception between you and your partner.

## No Strings Attached

"No strings attached" has to be the mantra for the beginning of a relationship. It will make a man feel comfortable and even flattered, because he will think that you want to be with him just for himself and the fun you have with him, and everyone likes to think that other people have fun around them. As soon as there's any 'predatory' feel to your attentions to him, his antennae will be abuzz with warnings.

I keep repeating, but it is so critical - his instinct is always to run in the early stages unless he's already totally infatuated with you. Take your cue from the way he expresses his feelings. If he's ready to start talking about the future then you can follow suit, without going overboard. It's in your own interests to keep your mind in the NOW. Don't create too many fantasies before you really get to know him. Cultivate an aura of temporary attraction, you'll find it easier to stay in the seductive role and you can act as if there are no long-term expectations, even if every brain cell is screaming for commitment! You will convince the commitment-wary man that he is not in danger of losing his beloved sense of freedom. Besides, you'll have more fun!

# CHAPTER TEN

## Donna: From Lust to Love

### *Progressing From Eros to Agape*

*Loving is mutuality; loving is synchronous attunement and modulation. As such, adult love depends critically upon knowing the other.*
Thomas Lewis, Fari Amini & Richard Lannon, *A General Theory of Love*

Moving from passionate, romantic love into real partnership was the next part of my journey with Paul. I must admit my definition of love was colored by my addiction to romance - the frosting on the love cake. I still have many triggers - a song, a slow-dance, a word, a scene from a movie, touching him, just looking at him - which evoke romantic feelings.

There are logical explanations of my chemical reactions and full-blown sensual seduction of Paul. I remember asking my gynecologist if my "going into heat" at my age might be injurious. She just laughed and said, "I suggest you go home and use it!"

The unique part for me was that *eros* lasted almost three years. Why? Because much to my surprise, Paul moved in and I was confused by that, because I had believed my own 'stay-in-the-now' seduction story. But Paul, the English Beta Male, was reticent in verbally expressing the dreaded three words, "I love you" in his normal voice, so he'd use comic voices as a way of keeping it light. Rather than suffer, I decided this was the perfect way to go; continue to stay in the Now and perpetuate my blissful state of *eros*.

Just one huge problem - the intensity of *eros* began exacerbating my heart arrhythmia. I then had valid reason to retire into *agape*, where I could relax. So began the serious training period for Paul. I started the Paul and Donna Mutual Appreciation Workshop. I began by saying, with a giggle, "I like you, Paul," to make a little joke out of my need for his expression of love. He went along with the joke and I let it continue for a long time. It was easier for him to be ironic and make light of his feelings than to express them, and I understood that. Eventually he found the word "love" less threatening and he evolved into being able to express his feelings.

My definition of *agape* love is choosing the highest good for the other person. This motivates cooperation, respect and appreciation, thereby transforming the soul. I also believe that only time and life experienced together (I like to call it T & M – **time and materials**) will define the many love petals on the partnership flower. I still constantly feel love for Paul, and I feel that love is the foundation of our day-to-day partnership. ***The giving is the getting.***

*People act differently when they're in love with different people. We tend to match our expressed interests and preferences to those of a desired individual.*
Geoffrey Miller[55]

---

[55] *The Mating Mind*, p.419

## Love

What is love? Let's try to define one of the more complicated words in the language. It is a chemical reaction that takes place in the brain and affects every part of your body. It's a physiological cocktail of symptoms that adds up to what we call 'love', a release of endorphins, adrenaline, proteins, hormones and other powerful reactants that might be controlled substances if they occurred anywhere but within our bodies, they are so addictive and mind-altering.

Love's effects touch every organ in your body and make you feel like someone else. It is Nature's way of helping us make attachments with mates that will last through the raising of offspring. In other words, the science shows that love's physical effects are a biological incentive for women to pursue the mate of her choice, and for the man to feel that he wants to stick around and make sex even better than it would be without love.

If that's too biological an explanation of love, feel free to think of it as "an eternal connection of two ethereal Selves, meeting as pre-destined in the Book of Fate, bound to go on together through eternity, soul mates for all time."  Or think that you are made for each other, that nothing before or since has compared to this love you feel for each other and that it will never change and never die.

My first wedding ring had "Forever" engraved on the inside. Ironically enough, I used the same ring for my second wedding too! Despite that, I do think of Paul as a soul mate. Whatever keeps the wheels turning for you. But when your passion fades and the sound of his footstep on the stair doesn't drive you into juicy anticipation you might wonder how this could happen to such deeply devoted sexual lovers.

Why is it that the symbol of initial love should be an arrow through the heart? Because it expresses the pain and the changes that love causes. It's like the sharp thorn on the beautiful rose. You will never be the same, once you have been in *eros*. It changes forever the way you see the world, the way you react to people and the way you think about yourself. Not just while you're in *eros*, but forever after.

While you're experiencing *eros*, your eyesight changes, your senses of smell, taste and hearing change, you lose your concentration, every thought reminds you of him. Every time you think of him, your heart rate changes, you get a hollow feeling in your belly, your eyes dilate and you perspire just a little more than usual. Men say they experience the same feelings. I hope they're right; it's a glorious biological state.

**Lucky in Lust**
You're probably thinking that's not love, that's lust. Well, it's actually lust in the cause of love, which is the socially acceptable face of lust. In our society, lust in any cause other than love is somehow sullied and dirty. It's seen as an obsession with bodily functions that have no place in polite society. All those things we hide behind curtains and frosted glass that are too 'smutty' to be mentioned in polite circles. We shy away from public conversation about anything that goes on "down there". The same goes for talking about lust as the human trait it is. Sexual lust is no more perverted than lust for money, yet one is shunned as bestial, while the other might get you a Cabinet position. So if you don't like the word "lust", use "love" if you wish.

I wrote the following poem to Paul in a state of full-blown *eros*, with all its forces pushing me into an incredible state of vulnerability and sexual ecstasy.

### Aries to Aquarius, Standing Up

Tongue tied,
vacuous
abstract noises,
relieved with giggles and laughter.

Stumbling,
cutting corners,
another bruise on my hip.

Forget the vinegar,
Forget the sugar,
Forget sleep.
Am I that tender snag in the forest?

## Aries to Aquarius, Lying Down

Slipping, sliding
into the
warm, delicious
aqueous coating of honey.
The Taste
The Smell
The Feel
of sweet primal ooze.
Pushed,
pulled by the fire.

If there is a place,
this is the place;
the place of freedom.
Freedom from the bitters of desire.
To celebrate desire.

Body/soul/Moebius strip
isolates the clock,
forbids the past,
forbids the future.
The celebration of The Now.

Quieted mind.

> Tantra flows through the warm fluids
> under the tender new moon.
> Freedom.
> How beautiful I am!

## Pulses Racing

So here you are, feeling the physical effects of all this lustiness and you want to experience it over and over again. That is *eros*, and it's the first thing you feel for someone to whom you're attracted. You will be physically attracted first, before all the other warm, fuzzy feelings take over your mind. It's all chemical and biological. That's why a simple touch on a man's arm can set his pulses racing.

## Choose Your Position

If you're an adult, it's your choice whether or not you should give in to your feelings of lust/love. Of course, the way women are programmed emotionally is different from men when it comes to sex, so it really is up to you to draw the boundaries, create a timetable, go at your own speed. If he pushes you too hard, too soon, it's a warning sign to you to check this man out a little more before you commit yourself any deeper. Part of the love that grows after the heat of lust is passed is grounded on respect. If you don't foster that respect from the start, you stand little chance of gaining any later.

## Don't Look For Yourself

Remember that what you feel for this new man in your life is special, but not unique. Until you get to know him better, you don't know too much more than the superficial - the way he dresses, the smell of him and whether he has a nice smile. That's no basis for a love that lasts beyond *eros*.

Try to remember that those Hollywood love stories are rarely about people that really *know* each other. Check it out, you'll find that in almost every case, it's all about purely physical attraction. And I'm guessing that most single women and men, if they were honest with themselves when they were looking for someone, would probably find that the ideal person they envision is a clone of themselves. But the ideal partnership is made of two people that complement each other, not feel, react and think exactly like each other. Everyone lacks some skill or trait that can be supplied by another person, that is the essence of partnership of the two differing brains.

## Real Needs Begin to Emerge

Partnership is about emotional connections and compatibility, and love can transform you, but you must be realistic. Unfortunately, at the beginning of most new relationships, women tend to only show their best and do not talk about their real needs. After *eros* begins to wane, marriages and partnerships are most threatened when the real needs of partners begin to appear.

You've heard married couples speak of the seven-year itch and even the three-year danger period. Perhaps these are the most dangerous stages, but whenever the 'when' comes, watch out! I felt that I deceived Paul when I changed horses mid-stream after *eros* wore off. I was embarrassed to tell him what I really needed. I have had a history of expecting men to give me magical sensual pleasure without communication - without my telling them how to do it. It is a fantasy. Most men want to know how to please women, but all women are different, so how can a man possibly know what to do without our telling him?

To a man, that is some kind of voodoo - he's going along in his own way, going with the flow, trying to please, but he is not a mind reader. His is not a woman, so he probably lacks the feminine sensitivity to emotional nuances that signal unmet needs and dissatisfaction. He has not been trained in that art, which comes so naturally to women. Cut him some slack. He is not to blame. Tell him what you need. If he wants to be with you, he will find a way to try to satisfy you. After all, up till now, he hasn't seen the real you, so he doesn't really know you from Eve. You've been on your best, most seductive behavior, creating your own mating display to dazzle and stupefy him.

If you're a man reading this, you might encourage her to talk about how to pleasure her. If she hasn't done so, remember this is not just her insecurity, but a western cultural syndrome. Women fear that talking about it might endanger your mysterious erection and your fragile male ego. Reassure her that you can handle advice without losing interest, especially when it's such vital advice for both of you.

## *Eros* Is Not Meant to Last

My experience with *eros* is that it began to wane soon after Paul said he loved me, and after the wedding vows I took with my first husband. Go with the flow, but always keep in the back of your mind that you are experiencing a severe chemical reaction and it will wear off later. Your entire body would go up in flames if you were always in *eros*. That's why, after a while, the heat of passion and lust begins to wear off and you don't think about his body night and day. It's the time when decisions are made that will affect the long-term relationship.

You've come through the period of *eros* and it's nesting time, so you enter a new period of love called *agape*. It's the long-lasting love that has less to do with radical swings in body function and temperament. It's that comfy, cozy feeling you have together, as if you're two really, really good friends, who also happen to be having sex, but perhaps less than you used to. This is the love that can last a lifetime, if the groundwork is done right from the start.

## The Young and The Wrinkly

*Eros* is not the time to be really considering the future in too much detail. You and he are in no condition to make plans; when you are 'crazy' about each other you are literally not in your right minds.

You must allow reason to return before making life plans. That's what an engagement used to be for. It was the cooling-off period, after the frenzied kissing of a gloved wrist in the hallway, when the servants' backs are turned - you know, all that Victorian-era heavy breathing, and lusting after a shapely ankle. People were so carried away by unrequited passion, that their fevered sleep would impel them to marry the object of their *eros*. That's still true of many young marriages. Here are two inexperienced young people in the throes of full *eros* and they "know" that they were meant for each other, so they go off and get married right away.

But before we wrinklies get too smug, it works that way for everyone in *eros*. In fact, the more desperate you believe yourself to be, the more likely you are to grab at the one straw of marriage that comes floating downstream towards you. Don't do it! You don't know him, he doesn't know you. You're lusting after each other. OK, make up your mind whether or not to sleep together, give it a whirl for a while, then start making plans once you know each other better. You must try to keep your mind in "the now" - taking it day by day, without any thought of a future together. Just remember the condoms!

## Moving In?

But perhaps we should stay with the present situation. *Agape* can wait until you have found out whether or not you think he might perhaps be a man you could settle with. If you're both in *eros*, he won't be thinking of the future. That tends to happen later in the game for men. Women experience all the joy and pain and ecstasy of *eros*, but it's also in our nature to always have that *agape* clock ticking away somewhere in our brains. We are made to be nest makers and it's an expression of our love for a man that we give him the opportunity to join us in the nest.

That could mean marriage, if you're more traditionally inclined, or simply living together as a means of testing the waters of full-time companionship, if you're willing to risk it. It's all relative to your religious, family and community norms and whether you want to adhere to them. He too has a need for stability in relationship, no matter how the Male Mask may hide it. He may not want to talk about it as readily, at least not until something happens that makes him have to look for a place to live.

"How about if I move in with you?" he might say one day, and if you've been harboring fantasies of the two of you setting up house together, that will sound pretty good. The other way is for you to suggest it, when the time is right, and that's also a tricky one. What often happens most naturally is that one or the other starts leaving articles of clothing at the other's home. If nothing is said, before you know it, there is mutual comfort in that kind of domestic sharing.

## The Lottery of Love

There are people who will complement your skills and traits with theirs. There are men out there whose pheromones will always turn you on. There's someone out there, in fact there are thousands of people out there, who will appreciate your sense of humor or your practical side or your love of animals. There are even those rare people who know from the start that they can live happily ever after.

Of course there are plenty of people who are pretty darned good candidates for partnering every one of us. The old saying that there are plenty more fish in the sea is so true - for everyone. A friend of mine in the real estate business says no matter how good that property looks, no matter how much you want it, it isn't the last one, there's always another. That is even truer when it comes to people. There are six billion of us on the planet now. Don't give me that "there's only **one** true soul mate for me" stuff. There are millions to choose from, and if you have the attitude that you can have any one of them, you'll do just fine.

## Chemistry Is Great, But...

So how do you know when that man is the right one? Nobody can tell you who's right for you, but there are certain qualities you begin to notice in couples that may be clues to success. With the rare exceptions when opposites attract - an adage that is not as true as some would have you believe - most young people like to find similarities between themselves, rather than opposing views and tastes. A couple that intends staying together must share at least some of the things that are important to them; similarities of mental, emotional, political, sexual and spiritual traits and preferences are all valid reasons for considering someone as a partner.

## Similar Attributes

Have you ever noticed how many young couples have similar physical attributes? Chins, eyes, height, weight, age - there are countless qualities that can ring your bell. Many of us are unconsciously looking for ourselves, even though hardly anybody knows herself, because we feel we are the ideal roommate for ourselves and want to be with someone who shares our likes and dislikes. Then there are the similarities between, say, someone's male partner and the woman's father.

People also tend to be attracted to those who look like other loved ones in their lives, such as parents, siblings, even ex-spouses. One theory is that we all tend to look for our parents in a partner[56], regardless of our parents' merits as people. What are called *limbic attractors*, connections in our brains that are formed by our own early-life experience, form our decisions later in life. We become accustomed to certain qualities in our parents (who form the earliest and deepest attractors) and our domestic lives, and our emotional patterns are set on our impressionable, young minds.

---

[56] Thomas Lewis, Fari Amini, Richard Lannon, *A General Theory of Love*, p161

Later in life, the connections still exist, giving us preferences in choosing mates who most closely match our prototypes. We go with the familiar, or a version of it.

## Ghostly Lover

Then there's the "Ghostly Lover", a Jungian term,[57] which for me means the fantasy person who combines mostly physical traits that are shared by others that have influenced us, such as teachers, parents, film stars, a first crush, etc. Everyone, at some point in their lives, has a picture of who their perfect lover would be. That is our Ghostly Lover, against whom all others will be measured. I know I had an image in my virgin mind of my perfect man, and my first husband came close enough to it for me to marry him. That turned out to be a major mistake. As time goes by and we become more experienced, we are more willing to settle for just some of those qualities, rather than the complete package. It is rare, but wonderful, when a person finds the complete package in someone else, but don't hold out too long. It's more likely that some compromises will have to be made in whom we choose to love.

## The Language of Love

In his book, *The Five Love Languages: How to Express Heartfelt Commitment to Your Mate*, Gary Chapman writes about the everyday ways that love can be expressed in long-term relationships. He identifies them as:

- Words of Affirmation - unsolicited compliments, encouragement and a kind word.
- Quality Time - togetherness and connection; listening to each other; having fun and exploring new activities together.
- Receiving Gifts - treats or cards for no reason; the message that your partner wants you to know he was thinking of you.

---

[57] M. Esther Harding, *The Way of All Women*, Harper Colophon, 1975

- Acts of Service - cooking, washing of fixing the car and other everyday jobs can be acts of love.
- Physical Touch - holding hands, especially in public, a hug, a kiss and making love are all ways of communicating love.

Regardless of why and whom we choose, raw chemistry is great at the beginning but all chemical reactions have a life span. Sooner or later the chemistry won't be enough and conversation with true communication will become more important. You'll begin to find out more about each other, what each of you misses of your lives **before** you met and where your true interests and enjoyments lie.

You might want to go to a peace march, he might want to go to an auto race. Over the weekend, you might want to go dancing with him, but he'd rather go camping. As time goes on and you spend more time together, your tastes will tend to merge; it's how humans form bonds that keep us together[58]. You may find something compelling about Puccini that you can't get from Shania Twain. He may not be as interested in stamp-collecting as you are, and you may not be into growing organic tomatoes like he is, but sooner or later, you will find some activity you can both feel passionate about.

### Embrace *eros*, anticipate *agape*

Permit passion in your life, and know that if you listen to your deepest feminine intuition, you will know when and with whom partnership is right for you. Don't give in to fear or desperation in finding your partner; trust your feelings and use your common sense. I have made many mistakes in my life and I've spoken to many women who regret some of their decisions in love, but I also know that when it works, partnership is the most glorious reward for all the trials we go through.

---

[58] Geoffrey Miller, *The Mating Mind*, p.420

It may be easier to give up and live alone, it may be easier to make excuses, but I really believe that by doing the work of being in true partnership, I have been able to make my partner's life better, as he has for me. We are both fuller beings.

When women do that, when they make those little changes in men's behavior through guidance and seduction, using their knowledge of current brain science, the effects ripple out into the world and, if you have children, on down into future generations. Paul and I think that partnership, from domestic to political, is key to the sustainability of our species. So those ripple effects of the effort we put into forming our own loving and creative partnerships form the foundation for culture-wide change.

We can save our next generations from being victims of the choices of disempowered women by starting at home, creating precedents and inspiring others.

# CHAPTER ELEVEN

## Paul: From Lust to Love

### *The Rake's Progress to Partnership*

*Good relationships usually develop slowly over time, growing out of the thousands of mundane interactions we share each day.*
John M. Gottman[59]

After fourteen months, I moved in with Donna and began the long climb out of emotional shutdown and fear of commitment. It was a dramatic shift from *eros* to *agape*. Now that we were together every night we could have sex any time we wanted, without having to commute. But, guess what, the drive to make love every time we saw each other went away. I was no longer turning up at the door with an erection; I was coming straight home from work, dirty and tired.

---

[59] John M. Gottman, *The Relationship Cure*. Three Rivers Press, 2001. Filled with practical advice on repairing and maintaining relationships in marriage, with children and siblings, and with co-workers.

There was still the outdoor bathtub in which I could soak and in which Donna would sometimes join me. There was still the excitement over what she had done during the day, especially when she was working on her twenty-foot canvas mural that ran along two walls of the studio. There was still occasional poetry. But there was also the inevitable cooling of raw desire. When we made love now, it was better than it had been in the beginning, because we knew each other's bodies better, but it was less often and less urgent.

In exchange, our love deepened, our commitment to each other increased, we became more alike in some ways as our interests merged. Donna began to suffer some health problems and we dealt with them together, we relocated together, traveled together, wrote our first screenplay and book together, managed a bed-and-breakfast inn together. Everything became a joint project – the most fearsome and satisfying part of a committed relationship. As we write this book, we are with each other twenty-four hours a day.

It's not always smooth sailing, of course, but the joy in our partnership is so much more than the pain. To counter our tendency to get "too busy" to make love, which is too prevalent in committed relationships, we have told our friends not to call on Sunday mornings. **Sunday Sex** is our way of keeping at least a weekly date to make love. It's not spontaneous, but we get all the great sensations and the renewal of intimacy that comes from the physical side of partnership.

I remember when Donna announced, at an award ceremony dinner, her idea of launching National Sunday Sex Day, a cheer arose from the men in the audience, as they threw their napkins into the air in celebration!

## The Unknown

What is man's greatest fear about a committed relationship? Loss of identity as a unique person, as a man, as a free agent. We men all know that once we enter into a full-time relationship, we will be different. We don't know **how** different and that's the real fear – the Unknown. It doesn't matter whether we're dating exclusively, living together, engaged or married, once the commitment barrier is passed, the changes will begin.

*I'm from the old school. I don't have a feminine side. I've been trained to be a male too long. But after 40 years of marriage, I realized that my life is more secure if I get in touch with the* wife *side of myself. All that takes is remembering what she likes and what she doesn't like. The wisest men give in early. They are able to measure in an instant what is important and what's not important.*
Bill Cosby[60]

One biological effect that few men know and might be alarming for them is that, when he has been partnered for a while, a man's testosterone level begins to drop. It's part of the 'civilizing' influence of relationship, a transformation from free-ranging big-game hunter strutting his stuff on the savanna, displaying to attract a mate, to protective and doting father and husband. We could call it domestication, which sounds a little better than being housebroken. (It is also true that, when partners get back together after being separated for a while, perhaps by a long trip, the man's production of sperm increases – a biological attempt to overwhelm any competitor's sperm that may have found its way into her vagina.[61]) The lowering of male hormone levels may occur at about the same time as the woman partner moves from *eros* to *agape*.

That's why Sunday Sex is so important for a continued sense of intimacy and romance, and Donna says I whistle and sing for the next few days, at least through Wednesday! So pay no attention to

---

[60] Bill Cosby, *Bill Chills* by Ana Figueroa, AARP Magazine, Jan-Feb 2004.

[61] Geoffrey Miller, *The Mating Mind*, p.231

hormone levels and such, just commit yourselves to continuing, regular lovemaking.

## When *Eros* Changes To *Agape*

*Eros* is when nothing matters more to the two of you than seeing each other again and satisfying the craving for the endorphin rush of lovemaking. It's the period of obsession that can blind us to most of our partners' faults for a while.

When a woman returns to normal and becomes a saner person, less obsessed with her lover's body and more concerned with his character, she may want less sex, more quality talking-time and more expression of feelings. As the sex drive dwindles in her and they make love less often, the man's testosterone levels will begin to drop and he too enters the state of love called *agape*, when two partners are settling into the tenderness of togetherness. For the woman, that is when the man is under the microscope. It's time for him to be more conscious of his behavior, if he intends to continue this relationship.

If the relationship means anything more to him than an excuse for getting his jollies, this is a critical time in its (and his) development. He is being scrutinized for his suitability as a long-term partner. Regardless of whether or not he intends, or has even considered, having children, or even if she is beyond childbearing, the natural biological progress of the relationship dictates that the woman act as if she is preparing to mate and rear her young - with his help.

To do that, she must be as sure as she can be that he is physically, emotionally and mentally fit for the job. The problem may be that she misreads his displays as being the true Him, when she is only seeing his Male Mask. If she feels that this man is for her, but she has misgivings about certain traits (how could she not?), she needs to be sure she is seeing the man within, using her innate, seductive Feminine. It is only when a man feels truly at ease with a woman that he will finally let her see behind the Mask.

## Acceptance and Reciprocation

I surrendered to Donna's seduction, won over by her Alpha Female sensuality. I recognized myself as the Beta to her Alpha. But she needed me to maintain my masculinity to be a partner in the relationship. I'd been a sea captain and a contractor, so I had my share of manliness, but I had never thought of myself as an Alpha Male. I'm one of those Betas who is unassertive and easy-going, without a leadership bone in my body, but with an independent streak. So my role of being the receptor in the seduction was fine with me most of the time, as long as I didn't feel railroaded. Donna was very careful not to cross that line, or was adept at redrawing the line without my noticing!

It was grand theatre and I was one of the stars. Now, as we entered a committed relationship, Donna found herself wanting me to be more assertive, which isn't my natural style. I've never felt that being a man depended on being a leader or organizer. That's for Alphas, and without them the world would be very different. No doubt we'd be less culturally and scientifically advanced, but perhaps there would be fewer wars and the planet would be in better condition. Impossible to say.

With her Alphaness receding and my Betaness well-entrenched and reinforced by my role as the receptor throughout the seduction, it became a delicate balancing act that really taught us a lot about each other, our hot buttons and our boundaries. Happily, we were both able to make adjustments and compromises in creating a strong partnership. Now each of us knows what the other's strengths and weaknesses are. No Alpha is fully adept at everything they do, and all Betas have something they are good at. Over the years, we've worked all that out. I feel like a man, Donna feels like a woman, and together we have a partnership that works.

Here's a simple rule, which many men do NOT know and which I was finally able to learn: Sincere Reciprocation. If Donna says "I love you", she wants to hear it from me. She actually wants me to say it first, of course, and I sometimes do. If she strokes my hair or puts her hand on my thigh, she wants me to do the same. This simple lesson on attentiveness has worked wonders for us.

## The "L" Word

Men have to learn from women how to express their emotions. It's a steep learning curve for men, whose brains are simply not wired the same way. But we can be taught by women how important it is that they hear from us how we feel about them. Compliments on your appearance, cooking and any other tool of seduction are of course expected, and men with any kind of training will be able to make them.

But he may take it for granted that you *know* that he finds you attractive. Men, while having almost as many hang-ups about themselves, just are not subjected to the same incessant body-shaming with which women are bombarded from early in their lives. He needs to be gently taught to say and do things that prove his affection. Simple things like making appreciative noises during sex may not be natural to him, but can be reassuring for you, so let him know that you would like him to vocalize a little more.

As a general rule, men will wait for a woman to say she loves him before saying it to her. The fear of rejection, of loss of face is even greater in men than in women, believe it or not. A man's whole self-image rests on his place in male hierarchy. It's just how we're built and how we have built culture. Also, most men don't feel the need to express their emotions constantly. It's not in their nature, unless women in their lives have helped them to do it.

To you women readers, if he can only say, "I love you too" in response to you, it's up to you to really *see* him and to figure out if you believe him or not, or if you have allowed him the comfort zone in which he feels safe. He has to feel that he can trust you with his emotions. I know that seems foreign to you as a woman who shares her emotions with friends all the time. Again, men just are not allowed by our culture to do that without fear of being seen as less than 'manly', and their brains are not made to connect to their emotions as easily as yours. So if the man in your life does express his feelings for you, be sure to notice it. Give him the reassurance in your smile, hug or kiss that you heard and understood him, and you appreciate his courage. Don't say that out loud, of course, and don't jump up and down and scream, "He loves me!!"

## You'll Both Begin To Feel It

If he can honestly express his emotions (and congratulations on making him comfortable enough to do so), an interesting thing will happen; he will begin to feel even more the depth of his love and commitment to you. Unexpressed feelings get suppressed, while those that are brought out are felt deeper and stronger, becoming part of who we are.[62] The changes that every manly man fears will begin to happen. He will become more dependent on your presence and his life will begin to revolve around you.

You can also express your love more freely to him, and he will not be as scared as he used to be. When he has done something practical and 'manly' for you, thank him and say you love him. He doesn't need to hear it as often perhaps as you do. And he may not think to say it as often as you would like. Unless there's a complete lack of loving attention from his side, don't take that personally. Once again, it's one of the differences between women and men.

## True Confessions

I have to admit for honesty's sake, that I am not the most demonstrative guy in the world (there's that old excuse!). I do tell Donna I love her, but nowhere near often enough. I happen to have a knack for accents and a wacky sense of humor, so in the past I'd often tell her I loved her in a French or fake English accent. It used

---

[62] George Weinberg, *Why He Won't Commit*, p.95

to be because of my fear of saying these words. While I don't do it now except very occasionally, it's only to impersonate the way I used to be. I'm no longer doing the funny voices, but I know I still don't say "I love you" often enough.

## The Trap

The stickiest part of commitment for men is our feeling of loss of identity and freedom. Before meeting a partner, a man pictures himself as a lone wolf, roaming the hinterlands of life; the prime predator, occasionally making a foray into civilization to make a killing, seize some prey, satisfy his hunger, then off he goes back to the wild; a creature of legend, respected and feared by all. No matter if he's a mid-level bureaucrat in Ohio or an Oregon lumberjack, that's the fantasy.

Now, he's met a woman who creates strange feelings in his chest, belly and groin. She's on his mind all day. He sees her everywhere, he remembers what she said to him last night. As he's preparing a flow chart, mending a water heater, taking a cab to the airport, or felling a fir tree, she is there with him, distracting and enticing. He can't share the real feelings he has with his buddies, because - well - they're his buddies and men don't talk about that stuff until it's really unbearable, and probably not even then. So there he is with this constant presence in his head and he's really alone, trying to figure it out.

He feels the urge to be with her all the time, but he senses danger. He knows there's a trap here somewhere, he can smell it, but he can't tell where it is or how deadly it is. It could be like a Roach Motel that'll hold him down until he dies or it could be like a humane trap he can live in for a while until he escapes, or perhaps a zoo cage where he might be treated well and given comfort. How can he tell?

## The Lone Wolf Fantasy

He needs to know that he's **not** going to be emasculated. Alpha Women **do** want to control their surroundings and their partners, but even for them, the major part of their attraction to men is the whole male thing. First and foremost, the physical differences - hair, voice, anatomy - and confidence, attention and dependability. When a man is that attractive to you, he needs you to let him know that those qualities are important to you and you will not 'take them away'. Yes, men *are* mostly that simple and fearful!

Again, it's all biological. The reason humans form partnerships comes from our instinctive urge to procreate, whether we're going to or not. So a woman's deepest primal need is for someone who seems to her to have the qualities necessary for fatherhood, and what could be more manly than siring offspring and being a good father? Men have the primal drive to ensure that their genes continue down the generations. Even if he's dead set against having kids (as I am), that is the biological drive behind a man's choice of a partner.

Beneath the Male Masks and civilized pretensions, we are male and female animals doing what animals do – eating, meeting and mating. So, although a woman will want to modify some of his behavior, she has to be careful not to erase his image of his own masculinity. That way, he can continue to have his lone wolf fantasy, maintain his manliness *and* be a devoted partner at the same time.

Let's say it again, painful as it may be for men to admit it - women are the civilizers of men. They train us to be the partners, housemates, husbands and fathers we are capable of being. None of us is born the perfect partner. As with everything else in life we must be taught how to do it by someone with the requisite knowledge, aptitude and skills. How could we possibly be expected to know everything about something we've never done, or never done successfully? And if we are going to be around a woman, unique unto herself, we have to know how to please her and get along with her. Who is more qualified to teach us that than the woman herself? Especially when it comes to sex.

## The Perfect Lover

It is impossible to jump out of the box at puberty and be the perfect lover. Yet men are under pressure to perform miracles and be an expert in something they know very little about without the right education. And where is that education to come from? In school we may be shown a condom on a finger, if the school board allows any sex education at all. Otherwise, it's Web porn, which will teach us nothing but that we have to be hung like a horse, that women are always HOT and there's no such thing as foreplay. No, the only place anyone can receive a real sex education is from a sex partner. Only she knows what works for her, just as only he knows his own turn-ons.

Most men are not taught or do not understand that all women are different when it comes to sex and pleasure. Our tendency is to treat every woman the same - it's that biological urge to spread seed around with as little thought as possible of the consequences[63], to keep it simple. Well, of course it doesn't work that way, unless the woman allows herself to be subjugated. So many women have so little knowledge of sex, even today, that they have never had an orgasm and don't even know about them! (We recommend a book about the fascinating history of vibrators, called *The Technology of Orgasm* and the documentary film inspired by it called *Passion & Power*[64]).

---

[63] Sarah Blaffer Hrdy, *Mother Nature*, p.83

[64] Rachel Maines, *The Technology of Orgasm: Hysteria, the Vibrator and Women's Sexual Satisfaction*; and Wabi Sabi Productions/First Run Features, *Passion & Power: The Technology of Orgasm*

Most men are not told that every woman likes to be touched in different ways. And even when he thinks he has figured out what his partner likes, he finds she's not constant in her needs, unlike most men! Unfortunately, most women are fearful about telling men how to please them. They're embarrassed, because it's not culturally acceptable to tell us what to do in bed. Also, they don't want to hurt our feelings, because men are supposed to know everything there is to know about sex. Ladies, let him know what you want and enjoy. Once he has had *mutually satisfying sex*, he'll want to repeat it!

The worst scenario is when marriage partners don't have sex at all, and have lost the intimacy it brings. Then there are those many marriages in which sex is just an exchange for household chores, or just a wifely duty, even in countries where women have a voice in their relationships. There's a sad quote from one of the interviewees in the book *Why Women Have Sex* that epitomizes the accepted sexual behavior in what might be called the "traditional" marriage, and we could hear this from wives in any part of the world.

"Most of the time I just lie there and make lists in my head. I grunt once in a while so he knows I'm awake, and then I tell him how great it was when it's over. We are happily married."[65]

Then there's a more humorous take on the problem from Rodney Dangerfield. "If it weren't for pickpockets I'd have no sex life at all."

## Adult Education

Men may have delicate egos when it comes to sex, because they're supposed to know it all. He might try the lame excuse that it puts him off his rhythm when his partner tells him what to do during

---

[65] Cindy Meston and David Buss, *why Women Have Sex: Women Reveal the Truth About Their Sex Lives, from Adventure to Revenge (and Everything in Between*. St. Martin's Griffin, 2010.

sex, not realizing that breaking the rhythm may be just the thing! Bu women have suffered too long from not daring to tell their men they need twenty minutes or so of foreplay. And they have been taught not to be pushy about how they like to be made love to, which can only lead to bad sex, unhappy partnerships, infidelity and divorce. Sex is a profound expression of mutual love when it is performed for each other's pleasure. When it's performed only so a man can get his rocks off, it shows her he has no empathy for her, he might as well be masturbating, and she definitely would be better off if *she* were!

There's more to a relationship than sex, of course, and men will have many lessons to learn, even if they've been in long-term relationships before. We advise them to treat every relationship as if it were their first and to be ready to behave in new ways.

Nobody knows how to behave in a culturally acceptable way until they are taught how to do it. Everything from potty training to conversation, from driving a car to table manners, every interaction we have with other people and most of our skills were taught to us by experts. Think of your relationship as a culture of its own, and think of yourself as the expert in acceptable behavior when he is with you. You're not really starting from scratch, but there will be many changes in the way he needs to act. It's the process of keeping him healthy, neater, more hygienic, more thoughtful of others, more careful around the house, more considerate and less reckless. You'll be helping him to grow up.

The training a man receives from his woman partner upon entering a close relationship is a part of becoming an adult human being. If he is prepared by his loving partner to relinquish some of his precious sense of independence and fragile machismo for the sake of the relationship, the guiding will be fairly painless. If he is not prepared to compromise, the relationship is doomed and may not even get off the ground, if the woman knows what's good for her.

## Not A Doormat

All this doesn't mean that a man should be the Private to your General, something all men dread in relationships. Regardless of how it feels, this isn't boot camp – make it clear that he is allowed to think for himself and he can drop out at any time in basic training! You have your own responsibility to the structure of the relationship. Being a partner is an active, not a passive, role. We're not saying that you should call *all* the shots in your relationship, but there are rough edges about every man that need smoothing.

While we advocate a greater active role for women in initiating and maintaining a partnership, men must play an active part. You don't want him to be a doormat and still expect him to be the man you need. He will feel less than a man in the part of your life that is most important to you. You will feel cheated out of the balanced partnership you expected, because you will be shouldering the load for both of you.

What happens in such a relationship is a shift of power away from balanced input and decision-making towards a matriarchal dominator model - the very antithesis of what you have been brought up to expect. That corruption of matriarchy is the flip side of patriarchy and has the same deleterious effects on partnership, because a true partnership is not guided by one person but by both partners.

The trick is to allow the man to maintain his independence within the partnership, asserting his will but not overriding you. The best partnerships are those in which two strong people can act together and alone on a creative collaboration of some kind. It could be a work project you do together, or fixing up a house, or raising children with full involvement from both man and woman. It's the responsibility of both parties to accept the give and take of partnership, compromising on the small stuff, while being honest with each other about misgivings and pleasures. Partnership is a constant checking-in with each other about the state of the relationship.

## Don't Suffer In Silence

How does that fit with the Male Mask that all men wear? How much of it will he have to shed to play his part in the relationship? Suffering in silence for the sake of a peaceful life will serve no purpose but to undermine the relationship. It's up to both of you to guide it. Don't take a back seat, or you'll lose control. It's your life and his being joined, so you can't just go along for the ride and expect to have the kind of relationship you want. *Seduction Redefined* teaches women to make their partners comfortable enough to be willing to work at a relationship. If he's not feeling comfortable around you, you're doing it wrong and it will not work.

At the beginning of a relationship, both of you are searching for the partnership that fits you both. You both have ideas, formed from previous experiences or what you remember of your parents' lives together. While a foundation of remembered success is useful, try not to remake your parents' marriage as your own. This is your life; it's why you left home. Be thankful for all the preparation your parents and others gave you, then form your own partnership.

## Famous Last Words

As far as I know, nobody has gone to their deathbed wishing they hadn't had such a happy marriage, that they hadn't told their spouses they loved them or that they could have had more divorces. Regrets about relationships are never about having done too well, so why not put everything you have into your relationship? It means surrendering a little on both sides to gain a lot, but just imagine if all your investments turned out as profitably! The important thing is to stay awake and to remember ***The Giving is the Getting.***

# CHAPTER TWELVE

## Donna & Paul: Partnership

*Personal Pointers*

*Love? What is love? I believe my* agape *love for Paul is layer after layer of respect, responsibility, kindness, creative collaboration and humor.*

Donna

*It is clear to me that partnership, deep listening, sharing and empathy are the key actions in solving personal and political problems.*

Paul

### Donna's Comments

Looking back, the one and a half years of seduction was the most exciting, creative, sexy, loving time of my life. Paul moved in with me, and the seduction and romance tone was set for many years after - candlelight, satin nightgowns, dinner dates, in fact we still call it a 'date' when we go grocery shopping. After all the ups and downs of initiating, your-place-or-mine discussions, theatrical, passionate lovemaking and moving in, here we are all these years later in a steady real-love relationship. Our partnership depends on how we co-create what we worked so hard to begin. So far, we've followed our own advice.

Since The Seduction, my dream of Partnership has truly manifested with Paul. I attribute our success to three major factors - **Communication, Creative Collaboration** and all the **Little Things** that make us both secure and *comfortable*. There's that important word again.

## Creative Collaboration

In doing our research, we found that the longest-lasting, happiest relationships are those where there is a creative collaboration between partners. For many, that means having and raising kids, with little left in common when the kids are grown. Creative collaboration means finding something in your lives that interests you, that requires some kind of creative thought, that you can work on and enjoy **together**.

Early on, we formed our creative collaboration. Paul agreed to write a book, *Brainlines*, based on my theory and research about the correlation of the vertical lines between people's eyebrows and right- and left-brain propensities. After that, we collaborated on a screenplay, a pesticide education non-profit (*Mow&Sow*), a peace organization (*BaringWitness.org*), a couple of interactive, outdoor art-for-peace installations and this book. We also continue to collaborate on a documentary film combining Baring Witness and this book, with one of its working titles being *Sex, War and Seduction*.

These creative projects have enriched our lives and our loving partnership. We are blessed. We get to pool our talents and work together on something that inspires us to do more. We bounce ideas and reactions around, we argue and laugh, and we spend most of every day together in our home office. Our long, long hours of discussion, writing and editing gave us both opportunities to understand and appreciate our strengths, our weaknesses and our male-female brain differences (see Chapter Seven), all of which is critical to avoiding blame and discord. Collaboration has been a great 'glue' for us as well as a learning experience.

## Communication

During our years of partnership I have combed Paul's past with "I want to know everything about you". His reality with his parents, his school, his friends, his teen years, his vacations, his first job, his first romance, his first sex - as well as the daily questions, "What happened at work?" "Whom did you talk with today?" ....all, all, tell me all. Even before I understood the biology of the male, I knew that 'guys' don't talk about life or its emotional impact. It was fascinating to find out how he and I react differently to the same situations.

In our communication from day to day, Paul is quiet and seemingly lost in his thoughts most of the time, but then, if I am patient, he surprises me with conscious and brilliant replies to my daily twenty questions. There is always the temptation to blame him for not bouncing back to me with answers to my blah, blah, blah with curious questions about my blah, blah, blah. Actually, what's really going on is his careful sifting process because he 'doesn't want to be wrong' and he really wants to help me. If I say, "I have something really important to ask you," he will listen and respond.

Now that I understand our biological differences, I can stop my blame game and whining because I really know that this man (like most males) does not have the biology or skills to fully discuss his emotion, let alone *my* emotion. It is up to me to resolve my dilemmas in my own female way - talking with girl friends, a therapist, or a family member, or reading self-help books.

Sure I can blah, blah, blah and that's a good teaching tool for him but I cannot expect him to solve my former or current emotional upsets, nor I his. We each try to take charge of our own lives and be a partner, not a parent. We help and support and advise each other, trying not to dictate what *must* be done, which would only breed resistance and resentment. I have learned that Paul will respond to intellectual or left brain issues, so I can get his attention more readily by the preface, "I have a technical question Paul." Aha, an immediate answer!

## He Aims to Please

It's super-important to understand and remind yourself that most men really do want to please the women in their lives, but they don't know how to do that until the women tell them how. This doesn't apply solely to sex, it's about everyday life. Men in general want to have as peaceful a domestic life as possible. Women tend to have unrealistic expectations of their husbands, expecting them to be sensitive enough to your subtle signs to know (as a woman is more likely to know) what you need. But he is not you, he is not a woman, he has probably not been taught how to be that observant, he is bemused by you sometimes and is probably not capable of being as empathetic as a woman.

What happens all too often is that women will feel unloved by their man (whom they once expected to be Mr. Perfect), they will expect men to sense it and will blame them when they don't. That can foster dissatisfaction, disillusionment and divorce. We must understand the differences that make men and women the perfect team when those differences are used in conjunction.

## The Little Things

There are always the little everyday things that couples can share and keep the 'glue' strong. Here are a few of our favorites:

the smell of onions or garlic sautéing
front hugs and back hugs at least twice a day
kisses on the forehead, the hands....or just plain kisses!
the shared bathtub
a back rub

homegrown vegetables
touching, hugging and cuddling
a clean windshield
Sunday sex
shared laughter
turning off the phone
the 30-second kiss!

There is always time for a kiss, a hug, a "love you", a "missed you", a squeeze, a favorite meal, a love note, a flower. Just one moment of caring will validate your caring. Too simple? No. Women feel good when giving. Again, *The Giving is the Getting*, and try not to measure the response – trust that you will be repaid in kind.

## Older Woman, Younger Man

When I kissed Paul, I didn't have my bifocals on and because he had gray hair I had no idea how old he was. As I said earlier, the seduction of Paul was an intuitive one and not a calculated one. Our age difference was not made much of earlier in the book because Paul and I believe that no matter what your age, the biological rules are almost the same and are not a deterrent. No matter their ages, partners need to know the little things that make each other comfortable.

By staying in the Now, my seductive and sexual passion in the beginning drove me further and further into our partnership world. Our sex, laughter and shared politics were so positive that the value judgments of the outside world about our age, and all cultural thoughts such as commitment, marriage, money or forever became much less important. We were totally free to enjoy each other.

One of women's great fears in Western Culture is that aging will somehow destroy the power of our Feminine. Of course, this is nonsense. My wrinkled, spotty, sagging body was not a deterrent to this twenty-years-younger, tall, handsome, intelligent, comedic and divine being. Physically, our connection was our freckly, sun-damaged skin and of course I couldn't hide my wrinkles (and they feel so soft!), so I wrote this poem to him:

### SKIN

As the animals graze the earth's crust,
you graze my lips
my neck, my belly.
Trust.

The skin which holds my
soul and sight,
holds the rounds and swells
up dark estuaries
of delight.

Within my rind,
my memory segments
recall,
the world's most vital disk,
the sun, the ball.

The sun moving, changing,
anxious to explore,
beneath
my devoted skin
saying no more, no more.

The sun fills the world with food,
my skin with ley lines,
to announce the pleasure.
(wrinkles don't rhyme).

Will or won't
the color, texture, discourage
a sleek old traveler

> who wants to curl beside you
> and dream?
> At your feet, perhaps.

**"Je t'aime, ich liebe dich, te amo...."**
My cultural damage got the best of me when I wanted Paul to respond to my "I love you Paul". For the first seven years he would not say, "I love you Donna". He didn't believe in clichés such as The Three Words or marriage. He continued to play the 'receptor', as I originally labeled him, to make my seduction safe for him. It was my fault that I was not more clever with the wording. In his comedic way he covered his fear of commitment by saying it in other languages, with a myriad of European accents, so I finally woke up and tested the waters with, "I like you Paul". His response was "I like you too" but he still wouldn't initiate. So then, I stopped all endearments for a couple of months - one of the old seduction rules - it worked!

Most problems arise from miscommunication. Men and women, including us, see the world differently, but now we know where each other's trigger points are and we avoid them, most of the time. We know each other very well, but we can still surprise and mystify each other at times, but we do not place blame or hold grudges.

Every day with Paul is an adventure for me. Our love layers are deepening daily. My dream life takes care of my mental philandering. I love Paul very much, in fact, when I'm gone for the day, I can't wait to return to him. I feel secure, loved and creative and we both still laugh at almost everything. That humor allows me once a month to tell him, because we have chosen not to marry, that I give him permission to leave me to seek another woman. It works, because I really mean it. To have an authentic partnership, **both** of us must be happy.

This is all fairly simple, and you too, can have just about any man if you try hard enough. It's not about degrees of physical appearance, intelligence, money or skill. Peel off that conditioned nonsensical media hype. You or anyone else can honor and promote the simplest pleasures into Technicolor, heroic acts of love and pleasure! What you like done to you, he will like doing - it's that simple. My respect and love for Paul increased exponentially by my belief that "the Giving is the Getting".

## Paul's Comments

So how is it being a Beta Male living with an Alpha Female? You have to remember that when we first met, there was some altered state of our minds going on, quite apart from the raging libidos we apparently both suffered from at the time. I was living alone in the country with two dogs and a cat, occasionally visiting the nearest town and scoping the field, while Donna had 'come into heat' and was actively seeking a lover.

My natural reaction to a beautiful woman asking me to kiss her was - to kiss her! And when the magic words were spoken, "No strings attached" that was certainly an added impetus to fall to the floor with her. Did I believe there would be no strings? I don't think I'd completely lost my innate male survival instinct and fear of captivity, so no. I had learned a few lessons from my wandering past, especially that sex changes everything between a man and woman. So I wasn't really taken in by the 'no strings' line, but I was impressed that Donna would have the presence of mind to actually say it. Her continued program of keeping everything in the Now showed a consciousness of the situation and her understanding of my fears.

## Younger Man, Older Woman

Was there no hesitation on my part, especially with Donna being 20 years older than me? Well, as you can tell, I wasn't a simple subject for her seduction. The age difference didn't, doesn't mean as much to me as it did to her. I was simply afraid of being caught in another commitment. Most men are, especially after a long-term relationship falls apart. But Donna knew and still knows how to make a man feel at ease. Through poetry, art, sex, theatre, intoxicating organic food and wine, and by never letting up the subtle pressure on me, she had me hooked before she even realized it, but I wasn't about to cave in too soon. The process was too delicious.

The constant soft barrage of poetry and phone calls, letters appearing in my mailbox every day, messages on my machine (cell phones still don't work out here in the countryside!) had me constantly thinking about her. I must say that sometimes I would have preferred not to be the target of so much attention, but that would have allowed my natural apathy to get the better of me. Far better and more stimulating to accept the onslaught and drown in the passion. After all, what was the alternative? Sitting in a downtown brewpub watching the game with the other single guys, eyeing women from afar and not being able to pluck up the courage to make a move? How would that be preferable to being the object of desire?

The sex was great, the conversation was stimulating, the food was gourmet and I was getting to know people in the local community on the rare occasions we actually went out to mix with others.

### Move In?!

I was having a grand old time, we were commuting alternately to each other's places, Donna was working on me and wearing her heart out from the constant roller-coaster effects of extended seduction of a skittish man like me. At some point, one of us had to say 'Enough' and give in to the pressure. It turned out to be me that reached the tipping point first. The house I lived in was about to be occupied by the owners, which meant I had to leave there. Where better to go than the warm center of seduction? So I sprang it on

Donna one day that I would like to move in with her. She covered her shock quite well, and as a low-income eco-artist, she could see the benefits of not having to drive or have me drive the twenty mile round-trip.

I should say that I *think* she was shocked. My decision to move in at that moment may have been part of the Great Plan, but I think that *even Donna* had not been as Machiavellian and omniscient as that!

## The Everyday Story of a Committed Couple

As time passed, the Erotic Adventures of Donna and Paul became the Everyday Story of a Committed Couple. That of course meant that we had to deal with many physical and psychological changes, including a drop in our libido levels and the need to compromise that comes with living with someone, especially someone with whom one spends twenty-four hours per day.

Our creative collaborations, which are part of our success as partners, have also been part of the test of our partnership. We are both independently-minded people, so when we reached a stage at which I was able to stop working for a while and Donna was able to put aside her art and activism so that we could dive into a collaboration on a book, it took a lot of adjustment. Add to that the fact that we decided to start work on the book *and* take a road trip down Baja California in our old Vanagon at the same time, and it could have been a recipe for disaster.

Flexibility, both mental and physical (I six-four, she five-eleven, in a VW camper!), was the key then and now. We have been able to take it a day at a time ever since, living in The Now while working together on projects that will have long-term effects on our lives. Does that mean our lives together are always perfect bliss? Well, let's just say we are all too human, with all the foibles that humans have. But the meshing of our world-views and humor help us to keep wanting more of each other, even as we need less of the 'stuff' the culture wants us to consume. We have a tiny garden of greens, tiny living quarters (by American standards) and an abundance of love.

## Succumbing to National Trends – Candace's Story

In the course of our research and travels, we've conducted interviews with people we meet. Here's an example of a partnership that is experiencing common problems. We interviewed Candace and she told us about some of the traps she and her husband had fallen into.

Candace: *I don't believe you know anybody until you've lived with them for at least five years.*

Candace's comment may be truer than we care to admit. We might like to think that by the time we move in with someone we know them pretty well, but partnership is a constant learning experience. Even years into a relationship, there are still lessons to be learned and the need to stay awake. We've all heard stories of long marriages that fall apart suddenly and "without warning" (see Paul's chapters!), or of partners who say "I don't know who he/she is any more." The truth is probably that one of the partners wasn't communicating clearly and the other wasn't paying attention to the signals. Time is not the critical component in knowing someone so much as making the effort to speak and listen deeply.

Candace: *I've gotten so focused on the kids, school and their sports. He's pretty good at verbalizing, for a guy, but I have to read between the lines. Like, he felt he was being left out of the picture, so he might as well not come home from work, because he wasn't being included. My interpretation when he kept coming home late was he didn't want to be included. Miscommunication. I must be very careful not to be distant and expect him to ask what's wrong - expect him to read my mind.*

Candace and her husband are a classic example of a relationship that is moving away from partnership. It's a national trend, hence the fact that nearly half of first marriages in the U.S. will end in divorce[66]. This is probably something you don't want to think about right now, if you're just starting out together. But forewarned is forearmed, as the guys say.

Candace is doing her modern, responsible suburban mother routine of ferrying the kids around to school, to soccer, to friends' houses, running a home *and* working as an executive. Of course, something's got to give, and she doesn't have time to cater to her husband's demands as well. He is retreating into his work, probably helping around the house at weekends, but otherwise being absent. The feelings of hurt and estrangement are building for both of them, and no doubt the kids are sensing the tense atmosphere. Candace and her husband have sex only occasionally, if at all, when they are both 'in the mood' and the kids are asleep.

### Intimacy - Sunday Sex and the Eldergasm

If Candace came to a *Seduction Redefined* workshop, she would be advised that Sunday Sex would go a long way to healing the hurt. We've already written about this, but it is so important to keeping a partnership alive. That is, scheduling a regular time at least once a week to make love, and for each to experience orgasm, whether or not it seems like too much work and bother. We can't stress enough the importance of a new mindset around sex. Sex creates guaranteed intimacy. It needs to be valued at least as highly as brushing your teeth, for heaven's sake, not something you do only when you're in the mood. It doesn't have to be Sunday of course, but we have told all our friends not to call us on Sunday mornings before eleven o'clock. It works for us.

---

[66] U.S. Census Bureau, Number, Timing and Duration of Marriages and Divorces 1996. Issued Feb. 2002

We understand that partners' schedules, kids, boredom, overwork and other distractions can wreak havoc on a sex life. That's when the physical side of love has to be scheduled, like every other family activity. Your mind and body will respond, once the commitment is made, once you begin to turn off the outside world and concentrate on each other.

*Sex is like vacuuming, a lot of work, but I like the end result.*
Anonymous

Again, Sunday Sex is the minimum – if you can find time to make love more than once a week, that's great. After all, for optimal health, younger men require at least two orgasms a week. And Donna, whose autonomic nervous system is not operating as well as it used to, has found the regenerative effects of multiple orgasm to be as health-giving as ever, even in her 80s! We call it the "**Eldergasm**".

You're probably thinking, "Sex has to be spontaneous to be good." Well, sorry, but that's a common cop-out and has more to do with movie fantasy than real life. Since when is "No Sex until we both happen to get frisky at the same moment and nobody else is around" better than "Some good Sex that isn't spontaneous"?

But most people do simply give up and wait for sexual inspiration to strike. One problem with that non-plan is that inspiration could strike when they're with someone else! If you're starting a new relationship, just bear this in mind for later. Right now, you know (we hope) how good it feels to make love and what long-lasting, positive effects it has. If you're young enough, you probably can't imagine a time when you both won't be ready to do it at a moment's notice. Hold on to that as long as you can! Nobody looks back on life and says, "I wish we hadn't made wonderful love to each other as many times as we did."

### Sex Tech 1A

We must just interject one clinical, physical fact about sex that is still clouded in secrecy and myth. The vaginal orgasm is much more difficult to achieve than the clitoral orgasm, and sometimes impossible. And seventy per cent of women have never achieved orgasm by penetration alone. The movie scene of the couple experiencing simultaneous orgasm after simple penetration in their first encounter is a myth. On average, a woman needs twenty minutes of foreplay before she is ready to orgasm from clitoral stimulation. So men, slow down, be tender and patient. Women may know that for most men having an orgasm is about as easy as tying a shoelace, but mutual enjoyment will take a lot more pleasurable effort.

### The Orgasm Box

Women's and men's brains differ in ways that help them act and react in their own ways. One example of the effects of those differences is sex. We believe that the biggest reason women take longer to orgasm than men is their greater innate empathic ability.

We like to say that a woman is never alone as long as she is sharing a space with another visible organism. (Donna says that women can see bacteria, but we'll keep this conversation above the single-celled beings for now!) So if a woman is never truly alone in a room or a bed with another person, and her empathy is always 'on', her brain cannot rest. Men have what we call the "Orgasm Box" (a variation on the Meditation Box and the Nothing Box), into which they can jump at a moment's notice and shut out input from the rest of the world until they reach orgasm. Women have to gradually find their way to a place where the brain allows them to concentrate on pleasure for a while.

That means that while her male partner is experiencing all the undiluted pleasure of pre-orgasm, with the occasional fleeting bit of performance anxiety, a woman is conscious of every movement, the spider's web on the ceiling, "why did he just make that noise?" "I hope he doesn't smell the garlic on my breath", "should I tell him to move his hand?" etc., etc. We think that's why it takes a woman so much longer to reach a state in which she can let go and enjoy pure pleasure.

## Women Need Romance

Donna believes that every woman has a triggering memory that can get her started on the way to pleasurable sex with another person. Every woman has some nerve ending that remembers when she first felt sexual pleasure in her formative years, and even if she can't consciously remember it, that nerve can. For Donna, her trigger is still Frank Sinatra, whose romantic ballads first encouraged her to think about love (and self-pleasure). That's why Paul carries an iPod-full of Sinatra-era ballads at all times, just in case!

## Men Need Sex

It's fairly obvious that men operate on a different sexual level than women. Hardly a month goes by without some well-respected politician or businessman is revealed as a sexual being who lost all common sense because of his overwhelming need for sex. When we quote our bumper sticker "Women Need Romance, Men Need Sex" we often hear protests that men are not all about sex, that they are spiritual beings with intellect and consciousness. Yes. Men are big-brained humans.

But humans are also just another species, powered by the same drives as every other animal, namely – ***eat to survive long enough to procreate***. Men are driven by sex, while women tend to be turned on by more romantic behaviors than men would display if it were not clear to them that that is what gets results. We'll say it again – males will adapt to the desires of the female in a natural mating system, that is, one that has not been perverted by millennia of one-sex dominance. That adaptation is why seduction works and why men can be guided into being perfect partners.

## The Perfect Relationship?

You will find, during the transition from dating to becoming a stable couple, that both of you have to change your ideas of what constitutes a 'perfect' relationship. Culture may supply the 'glue' of engagement and marriage, but after the honeymoon (often less honeyed than we might expect), what then? You both had fantasies to begin with, although women tend to have more expectations than men. Men pretty much prefer to 'travel light'. The woman might have her fantasy of the couple that shares interests and can almost read each other's minds, they're so compatible.

Both of these scenarios are unrealistic[67]. The man is always going to have to give up his dream of independent 'guydom', free to come and go at will, because, of course, that won't work in a partnership. He will come to realize that he won't be any less of a man if he makes some changes in his lifestyle to suit her preferences. And she will become more aware of the differences between men and women:

- he cannot read her mind;
- he doesn't think the way she does;
- he's probably unaware of the nuances in her body language and emotional signals;
- he does have emotional needs.

## A Lover and a Friend

As *agape* takes over from *eros*, your partnership will add layers of friendship to the love you feel for each other. That friendship adds strength to a loving relationship so that you can see each other through hard times. According to Alina Ruigrok, a relationship

---

[67] George Weinberg, *Why Men Won't Commit*, p.49

expert, the following list will help you tell if your partner is a friend as well as a lover.[68]

- You can talk to each other about anything.
- Your partner is always there for you when you need to talk to someone.
- You can always rely on each other when one is counted on.
- You have a permanent shoulder to cry on when you need it.
- You have many things in common.
- You accept one another for who you are.
- You listen to each other and consider each other's opinions important.

## Learning to Disagree

Inevitably, in any relationship, there will be arguments, usually when one or both of you feel you are giving too much for too little in return. It's at times like these when it is most important to keep the dialogue open. Men tend to put on their Male Mask when they feel threatened by a challenge from their partner, which may either infuriate the woman even more, because it seems he is not listening, or it will make her shut down as well – this time.

We advise men to beware the argument in which she has to back down before his Mask. Her pain and disappointment will come back to haunt him in some way, later on. She will store this memory away, and it will nag at her from within. It's a negative on his scoreboard. Far better to let the argument go to its conclusion. Try to listen deeply to each other's points without firing back knee-jerk, hurtful retorts for the sake of scoring points. Don't use the worst tactic of all, which starts "You always do this…" If there's anger, wait and discuss the issue when you're both calmer. A woman's

---

[68] Alina Ruigrok, *Building the Bond in your Relationship*, www.lifematters.com/building_bond.html

brain is powered by emotions, and memories linked to strong emotions are not forgotten.

Keep in mind that many men tend to avoid conflict in the home, if they can. It is the one place in the world where they feel they shouldn't have to prove themselves. They will tend to back off, shut down, leave the room, and assume the Mask. A woman at that point might translate his behavior as a sign that he doesn't care about her or the home or the matter at hand, and she may start counting the number of times he has walked out of an argument and say "He never talks to me." But for some men, it's the way they try to keep the peace. It doesn't necessarily mean he doesn't love you, more that he doesn't know how to argue with you. It requires finesse on the woman's part at a time when finesse is the last thing she is concerned about.

If he does stay around to argue, he may still put on his Mask and lash out at you from there, his bastion of safety in a hurtful world. If you know this man well, you'll know when he has assumed his other persona, perhaps sulking, perhaps shouting, perhaps bullying with his masculine power.

## Find the Genesis

Women, you don't have to buckle under to his Male Mask, because you know it's not who he really is. Reason with him to let him see the righteousness of your point of view; be prepared to compromise, as he also must. By compromise we don't mean giving up preferences that are dear to either of you, but being flexible in your attitudes, allowing change to occur where it doesn't involve feelings of surrender of your values. Try not to tear off his Male Mask or belittle him in an argument; the damage done will be difficult to repair and he will retreat from you and the relationship, deathly afraid of losing his masculinity.

Remember the feminine power lies not in force but in persuasion and seduction, which requires nurturing and a certain empathy.

When you know him well enough, you might be able to visualize the world as he sees it. He may just be irritating you with some habitual behavior that just drives you up the wall, and finally you can't take it any more. Try to think of what's behind that behavior; how did it come about that a grown man would leave his dirty socks on the coffee table? Is he doing it just to tick you off? Or is it a symptom of his unconsciousness? Or was he doted on by his mother, who always picked up after him, no matter what?

No matter how petty or serious the cause of the argument may be, you have to understand that he probably doesn't want to make you angry. Most men want a quiet life at home at all costs, so what would be the point? He's probably oblivious, and that's where the root cause of the disagreement comes from. He needs a nudge to wake him up, not a baseball bat upside the head. It's about empathy and nurturing again. When both of you can understand where the other is coming from, in behavior patterns, habits or points of view, even if you don't agree or would do things another way, at least you know what's causing the problem.

**This Is Not a Competition**

Both of you know how it feels when someone ridicules you or tries to humiliate you. This should never be what an argument is about. It should always be *on the subject*, not on perceived slights or mistreatments from the past[69]. In the emotional heat of an argument it's difficult not to try to score points in any way you can, but nothing could be more hurtful to your partnership. When people are willing to hurt each other just to win an argument, the trust that exists between them will erode. That can happen at any time during a relationship; when you're just starting out and don't

---

[69] Alina Ruigrok, *Building the Bond in your Relationship*, www.lifematters.com/building_bond.html

know each other well, or when you've been together long enough to know just which hurtful buttons to push. Either way, it's a bad sign.

Don't fall into the trap of saying to yourself "If he loved me, he would do such-and-such."[70] That kind of expectation means that you're relying on your partner to be psychic. Far better for you to ask for what you want up front. As you know by now, we want both men and women to tell their partners what they need.

## Adjust and Adapt

Candace: *We rotate, alternate. Jet Li once or twice, then I say, we gotta have a chick-flick. But we have found a common ground in the foreign films. If he wants more shoot-em-up films, I go to the kitchen and pop in when there's not blood oozing all over the place.*

We want to make it clear that you can't expect him to be a mind-reader and he can't expect you to be as wild as he is about the things he enjoys. If all went well during the seduction, you were bending over backwards to share his interests, to let him know what a good sport you are. He too, we hope, will have been showing up to support your choices. Well, don't be surprised when that changes as you settle down together.

Men can be resentful when they see what they regard as their independence slipping away, especially when that involves changing their habits. Moving in together changes everything. Suddenly, he is expected to be more 'grown up' and to make adjustments to accommodate your likes and dislikes. After all, you've probably been doing it for him since you first met, so now it's his turn.

We tell men to consider this every time they feel that they're making too many concessions. With any luck, and some hard work,

---

[70] Lynn Lott, *LifeMatters.com: Relating Myths*, www.lifematters.com/relatemyth.html

the woman he's with will be his best friend and the most caring person in his life. As with most situations in life, he must adapt to his environment, and his immediate environment now includes just the two of you, with your friends and acquaintances in orbit around you.

## Her Alone Time

Most women need independence too, meaning alone time. A woman's basic nature gives her an unconscious attachment to everyone around her. It's that nurturing drive, which some women may not feel as strongly as others, but it's there in her empathic brain. Put a man in a room full of strangers, people with whom he has no professional or critical need to make contact, and he will scan them, rank them in some sort of hierarchy, and be ready to defend himself against any danger they may represent to him.

Put a woman in that same room and she will also scan the room, but will sense different things; someone in pain; someone fearful; a man over there obviously suspicious of everyone else. She will need to connect with someone. So, as we said earlier, a man can be alone, or make himself be alone by entering his Nothing Box, in a room, while a woman can never be alone unless she is completely by herself. And sometimes, even in the most successful partnership, especially if there are children, she will need her time alone.

## Why Won't He Talk to Me?

Lastly, a common complaint we have heard from women in long-term relationships is the lack of communication with their men, especially those men who were dazzlingly articulate in courtship. Again, it can be partly because the time spent in raising children and at work is time that cannot be spent in conversation together. Also, there is an evolutionary reason that men who were highly verbal during the dating phase will be less so once the relationship is formed.

## Seduction Redefined

Male humans display their verbal skills as indicators of their intelligence and creativity, which are highly desired by females. So the poetry he wrote and the highly-charged and witty conversations during courtship were sexual displays to attract the woman, and once he has exclusive sexual access to her, there is less incentive to waste energy on sparkling repartee[71]. This is biological, not a conscious decision, so let's not assign blame.

What then is a successful partnership? It can be a complete melding of two separate personalities, each filling the other's needs, meshing perfectly and snug as Velcro. More likely it will be a mishmash of mistakes and triumphs, high and low, each partner gradually getting the hang of living with the other, until it doesn't feel as if there's any other way they could be happy. It could be a way for partners to pass their lives that feels comfortable and safe.

Any relationship that works for both partners is a successful partnership. Sometimes it won't work out, but every experience in relationship is a lesson that can help a future partnership. Every misunderstanding can evolve another level of love. Perhaps true love is the understanding of misunderstandings in a partnership.

Relationships are just the beginning for creating partnerships. If we can begin to create partnership in our own lives, perhaps we'll be able to see where it can help in the outside world – in politics, business and every human interaction. Perhaps if we start to think of a man and woman in partnership as one human being that just happens to be divided between two people, we can begin to see the necessity of the Feminine and Masculine combining their respective strengths for survival of the greater organism. Each of us has the Feminine and Masculine in varying degrees, even if one or both are hidden in order to conform to societal norms.

---

[71] Geoffrey Miller, *The Mating Mind*, p.382

If you extrapolate relationship difficulties into the global political scene, you begin to understand why nations are at war. The inability of the Alpha-Mask men in power to say "I was wrong" or "I made a mistake" has been one of the major causes for continuing conflict and xenophobia. Clinging to dangerous notions of the infallibility of Alpha authority lead us ever deeper into conflict.

Partnership, sharing, empathy, deep listening, cultivating the Functional Feminine and the ability of the men in power to drop their Male Masks enough to be able to see beyond their righteous anger will make a difference in the sustainability of our species. And it all starts with one woman waking to her Feminine power, understanding that men *want* to adapt to her desires.

# CHAPTER THIRTEEN

## Donna & Paul: Questions of Sex
### *Sensuality and the Redefining Woman*

*Any sexual myth does a disservice to the people who hear it by further eroding women's and men's sexual confidence, which is the key to letting go of inhibitions and exploring sexual pleasure.*
Lou Paget[72]

If you're an adult, it's your choice whether or not you should give in to your feelings of lust and sensuality. The way women are emotionally programmed is different from men when it comes to sex, so it really is up to you to draw the boundaries, create a timetable, go at your own speed. If he rushes you too soon, it's a warning sign to you to check this man out a little more before you commit yourself any further.

---

[72] *The Big O: How to Have Them, Give Them and Keep Them Coming.* Broadway Books, 2001

### First Date or Thereafter?

Sex early in the relationship—to bed or not to bed? It's a matter of personal preference and circumstance, but, if you're not just doing it because you want a quickie, you need to be aware of your goals. I know, it sounds boring and clinical, but spontaneous sex isn't always what it's cracked up to be. **It's important to stay in the Now**, and even to say, as I did, "No strings attached," but letting a lack of planning hijack your body to places you didn't want to go is no way to run a redefined seduction. Whenever you have sex with him, whether on the first date or at any point before true commitment, don't do it because you think of it as your only choice for keeping him. Do it because you enjoyed the sex play.

If you hope to make a lasting relationship with him, sex should be an outcome of your mutual attraction and decision. If he makes you think that sex is a prerequisite for any other sort of intimacy, if he tells you that **everyone** does it on the third date, you have to weigh the situation carefully and if it's OK with you.

No one can tell you what's best in your own case. Everyone is different and has different needs from a partner. If you agree that sex would be a good way to form a bond between you, it may be the right time to do it. If you're doing it only to keep him interested, think about why you're giving up control of your body to him. If you're in it for fun, go ahead, and don't forget that you can "use" him for your own pleasure—it goes both ways.

If you want to be the one to decide when the time is right to initiate sex, you are not alone, nor are you a prude or a slut. You have *Seduction Redefined* backing you up! There was a study[73] in which women were asked how long a man should wait before initiating sex while steadily dating. (By the way, notice that the question is about men initiating, not partners agreeing to initiate, or women

---

[73] Laurence Roy Stains and Stefan Bechtel, *What Women Want*,

initiating! Once you start paying attention to the bias, you'll see it everywhere, in scientific studies, in the way news is reported, and on and on!) Only 1% of the women answered "less than one week," a full 37% said they want him to wait between one and three months. Here's a really interesting figure: **25% said they wanted men to wait until they, the women, initiated.** That's a quarter of the women surveyed wishing that men would wait for them to initiate sex. There is no record of how many of those women have lived up to their own criteria.

If you're hanging back from getting physical because you have a feeling this relationship could really go somewhere and you're ready for an emotional rather than physical bond at first, or if you just want to take it slower than he does without alienating him, then you need a more gentle and truthful approach. Let him know that you'd like to continue seeing him and that a "No" now doesn't mean "Never."

### The De-erector

What if he's really insistent about having sex and you're not ready? How do you turn a man off? You can say, "No!" and explain that you're just not ready yet, that you need time to get to know him.

But the universal, all-purpose surefire method of wilting his ardent manhood, especially on a first date, is to start talking about marriage, moving in together, babies — anything that spells commitment. Unless he's a complete creep (in which case, get out of there), he won't just say, "Yeah, sure, whatever you want" and continue pushing you.

On a first date and until there is real commitment, a relationship is all about staying in the **Now**. Any mention of a future is going to be a turn-off for him. Be mindful that this is a relationship breaker, too. You won't just cool his ardor for the night, you'll send him running for the hills, probably never to be seen again. If that's OK with you, give it a try. Most guys will be zipping up their fly before you can finish the sentence.

**Your Move or His?**

I've been asked by men if women would see a man as weak or not having any "balls" if he waited for a woman to initiate sex. I think we can apply that question to all initiations between men and women, from the first approach, through sex to the marriage proposal.

The question itself indicates the pressure that men feel to perform to some nebulous standard of manliness, just as most women feel obliged to conform to stereotypes of femininity. You have to ask yourself the question— how do you feel when a man seems to be waiting for you to make a move? Is he just a wuss or does it feel good to have your feelings taken into account to such an extent? It could be that he's just waiting for that one little signal that you're ready to dance, or date, or have sex, or get engaged or ready for him to take command of the situation. Or it could be that he's ready to allow you to choreograph the seduction dance.

Would you think less of him because he's not rushing at you, erection to the fore, and taking control? If so, you need to understand more about men and their displays, and about your true, biological role in the mating game. And perhaps you need to look more kindly on the less assertive guys. Consider their past damage, consider the obvious depth of their sensitivity, and yes, consider their less-then-Alpha ego, and think how that might fit into your life. The assertive guys may look hot now, but once they're done with you, what then? The Beta Males are far more flexible and open to change through the influence of a loving partner. And the sex might even be better!

## The First Time

*Seduction Redefined* is all about debunking the myths that keep us separate and unsatisfied in our relationships. One of the most devastating myths is the all-American male-fantasy movie myth created by sex scenes in which the woman seems to have a vaginal orgasm from the mere penetration of the penis. Real women have a different story. Vaginal orgasm can be difficult, if not impossible, for most women to experience, especially on the first encounter.

Current research shows that only about 20% to 30% of women experience orgasm from penetration alone. The primary reason for this is probably physiological, rather than psychological. It seems that if the clitoris is more than one inch away from the vaginal opening[74], there is little chance of stimulation from the penis alone, and a lot of women are built that way, except apparently those characters in steamy movie scenes.

And the typical depiction of sex in porn movies, of men pounding away, fast and hard, is not the way most women enjoy sex, at least not until the final stages, perhaps. So men who have not been given advice by women on how to give pleasure have little chance of doing so. That leads to women feeling like failures, perhaps faking orgasm (as the majority of women have[75]) to move things along, and men feeling that the lovemaking wasn't quite up to the fantasy ideal.

> *It makes sense for a 'choosy clitoris' to produce orgasm only given substantial foreplay and emotional warmth, because this would reinforce only sex with males who have the willingness and skill to provide the right kinds of sexual stimulation.*
> Geoffrey Miller, Ph.D.

---

[74] Mary Roach, *Bonk*, Chapter 3. Fun book on sexual research.

[75] Shere Hite, *The Hite Report*, 1976 and 2000. The classic study.

So, the normal first few times with a new lover are liable to be less than 'perfect". It's nobody's fault, except generally the fault of our education in such things. The average scenario is that the woman will be the object and receptacle of the man's desire and pleasure and she will have to wait until later in the relationship to feel like a sexual equal. Our feminine nurturing qualities imbue women with an overriding need to pleasure their partners before thinking of themselves. That has to do with the brain differences referred to earlier, which cause such different 'timetables' during sex.

If the man has his orgasm first, he will be sleepy and in resolution, while she is left in a state of high energy with a need for sexual release. Normally she either blames herself for his early ejaculation or her own inability to have a vaginal or quick orgasm, or she says to herself, "I don't need an orgasm," or she masturbates. That's at least a healthy alternative, as long as she doesn't feel any guilt about doing it.

The tired old male notion of the "frigid" woman has a lot more to do with lack of education, lack of consideration on his part and other factors that keep women from truly enjoying sex, such as:

• **Sexual abuse**, including incest and date rape, is experienced by something like one in three American women. Enormous emotional damage, creating fear of intimacy, fear of men, fear of sex, and for those women who do manage to form a relationship, the possible fear of showing enjoyment of something that is either a painful or guiltily pleasurable memory.

• **The Pill**: For the past thirty years, researchers, providers and birth control pill users have acknowledged that the pill can cause a number of side effects such as decreased libido, sexual enjoyment and lubrication during sexual intercourse. The Pill is used by more than 80% of American women born after 1945 and affects a subgroup of 5% - 10% of them in this troubling way.

• **Fake orgasm**, women fake it for fear of looking inadequate, so as not to hurt their partner's feelings and to get the unsatisfying act over with.[76] This can become a habit, especially if the woman can't bring herself to ask her partner for what she needs or admit that she has faked orgasm in the past.

• **Pathological accommodation**: faking orgasm can be part of this condition, which causes the woman to subjugate herself damagingly to someone else's desires.

• **Lack of vaginal orgasm**: vaginal orgasm is only recently being seen as something less than the norm of sexual release, and may be impossible for some women, especially without understanding and guidance.

• **Lack of any orgasm:** a surprising number of women say they have never reached orgasm, vaginal or clitoral, during sex with a man, or during masturbation. Cultural mores, lack of knowledge and guilt about masturbation have a lot to do with this. Drug corporations are feverishly looking for the pharma-fix for what they call Female Sexual Dysfunction, a marketing fiction that will be hugely profitable for them and hugely confusing for women who may simply need honest guidance, not another drug for a phantom 'condition'.[77]

• **Male circumcision**: the lack of a foreskin necessitates greater friction for male orgasm, which encourages the 'porno pounding' style, rather than less athletic, more intimate lovemaking. Uncut men tend to hold you closer and want you to move less, and the cushioning effect of a foreskin is very pleasant, with less of the

---

[76] Sylvia de Béjar, *Tu Sexo es Tuyo*, 2005. Women can take charge of their sex life!

[77] *Orgasm Inc.* Filmmaker Liz Canner takes a job editing erotic videos for a drug trial for a pharmaceutical company. She soon begins to suspect that her employer, along with a cadre of other medical companies, might be trying to take advantage of women (and potentially endanger their health) in pursuit of billion dollar profits.

'scraping' that can occur with circumcised men.

•**Menstruation**: It can be painful, even debilitating. For many women and men it is embarrassing to even talk about, let alone think of having sex during menses. For some women, it can lessen the pain of menses. And for others, it is fine, just a little messier.

## Getting It Right

Given all these difficulties, is it any wonder that the most natural thing in the world – mating – can seem like a minefield to our species and its complicated cultures? Just don't feel bad if you don't "get it right" at first. It takes time to get to know your partner and even if you've had many partners before, everyone is different. That's what makes it all so exciting!

What if your first date did lead to the bedroom? Will it be a one-night stand, or more? Early sex may give a woman a feeling of being "used", but surely, unless you were completely drunk or stoned or he raped you, it should have been a consensual sensual experience—you were "using" each other. It is more important than ever to stay in the **Now**, not to let your fantasies take flight because you've slept with him. Your biology makes this your most vulnerable time as regards broken dreams and disappointment. If the sex was anywhere near great, the average woman (and the occasional man) tends to start planning for the future with this stranger she has slept with just once. For your own good, try to resist such fantasies.

If you've had sex early in the dating ritual, you are still a long way from building a lasting relationship. The sex may make it easier to seduce him, although once given it cannot be taken back. You will have lost some of your mystery, and mystery is a big part of seduction. But you can now give him what no one else can; your own special attention to his needs and desires.

Make sex your expression of love, not just passion, take it easy on the nest-building fantasies, make him comfortable, make it clear that you and he are partners in sex, and let him know what makes *you* feel good. When you feel good, he feels good, which makes the lovemaking better and you both feel better, and on, and on...

# CHAPTER FOURTEEN

## Donna & Paul: The Brain Science

### *Two Brains of One Mind*

*Essentially, men remember facts and figures, but women record not only the facts, but also every detail of the emotion that they're feeling.*
Louann Brizendine, *The Male Brain*

Since we became partners we have searched for the information that explains how two people that live together can sometimes feel like members of separate species, and yet they seem to work as one. We found that there are profound differences in brain structure between women and men. We also realized that that is exactly how it is meant to be, and that those differences are the strength of our species.

From the start, Donna was more impulsive and emotional than Paul, especially when she was in the midst of her seduction of him. Once they were living together and she came to him with problems he would try and fix them, and be alarmed when she thought that he wasn't listening deeply and didn't respond the way she thought he should.

It turns out that was all very normal for women and men. A man has the 'fix-it' part of his brain that makes him want to solve problems quickly. While he's doing that he may not look like he's listening. A woman needs to explain her problems in detail. It's how she deals with the emotional stresses of the day, which is the opposite of how a man deals with his stress – he wants to shut down, not talk, at least for a while. She just wants to verbalize everything so that her brain can process the information, which is puzzling to a man.

## Multiple Realities

We have learned in our own partnership that our cognitive dissimilarities have helped in our creative collaborations. Combining our two brains and their separate abilities has given us the ability to explore and explain far more effectively than if we were doing it alone. But it does take some knowledge, understanding and practice to get past the frustration and blaming of each other that so often occurs in relationships.

If your brain converts sensory input in a way that differs from another being, how can you know what the other sees, hears and feels, or how they react to similar sensory inputs? Einstein said, "Reality is merely an illusion." If our perception of the world is what makes it seem real, then how many realities really exist? Well, at least two. There's the world generally perceived by men and the world generally perceived by women.[78]

There's lots of overlap and there are many shades between the ends of the spectrum, so no absolutes here, but, if our brains perform in

---

[78] Louann Brizendine, *The Female Brain*. Three Rivers Press, 2006. *The Male Brain,* Three Rivers Press, 2010.

accordance with their owner's manuals without cultural interference, the male brain translates the world quite differently from the female brain, because of the structural differences.

You may have the feeling that your partner thinks differently from you, in fact you may not understand how she or he can each such different conclusions about the world. Sometimes these different processes can be downright annoying, and our responses can be damaging if we react to them impulsively, rather than understanding their genesis.

Brain research shows that the differences between women and men in brain structure and function are greater than were imagined even in the twentieth century. Where once a man might call his wife hysterical, or a wife might call her husband thoughtless, we would hope that they would now be able to consider how damaging those reactions can be. If we can pause in our condemnation of our partner and consider the reasons for their thought processes, we may avoid the emotional responses that can get us into trouble.

We have talked to many women and men about their relationships, and have lost count of the times that women have put down their male partners for acting like men. Many of the men we have talked to have more of a sense of humor about their inability to understand their female partners, but the frustration is evident there too.

### Complementary Abilities

Women's brains have more connections across the *corpus callosum*, the central divider between the brain's hemispheres than do men's. That gives women a more holistic sense of the world than men and makes them more able to multitask efficiently. Men have less sensitive auditory response, but startle less easily. Men tend to focus on one thing at a time, while women's attention tends to be more wide-ranging.[79] Women talk more, partly in order to process information, while men take information in and store it.

Women have a larger hippocampus, the area of the brain that stores emotional memories. Men have larger areas of the brain devoted to sexual impulse. Women have a larger area devoted to empathy, the ability to feel what others feel. Men have a larger temporal parietal junction, the part of the brain that deals with finding solutions to problems.

The frontal lobe is bigger in men for systems and organization skills, and denser in women for emotional control, judgment and planning. The female brain has a denser temporal lobe for language processing and comprehension and that, combined with the greater connections across the *corpus callosum*, allows for verbal fluency from the left and right hemispheres.

Again, there are always shades of gray when it comes to gray matter matters, and the brain is more plastic than believed only a short while ago. In the fetal stage, the sex of the brain is decided by the presence of androgens, and all the sexual characteristics are influenced by the amount of hormone production. Hence, the brain is on a continuum from masculine to feminine, and may not jibe with the outer physicality of the body from which we are assigned our cultural roles as women or men. The brain may be more feminine or masculine than that assigned role in the way its male and female structures are used.

Even elderly brains can change their neural pathways, given the right stimuli. Another variable is shown in musicians' brains. Boys who are trained in music from an early age form more connections

---

[79] Allan & Barbara Pease, *Why Men Don't Listen & Women Can't Read Maps: How we're different and what to do about it.* Orion Books, 1999

between the left and right hemispheres.[80] Their brain becomes more 'feminine' in its multitasking abilities.

The complementary perceptions, reactions and thought processes of the two brains working together have helped our species adapt to almost every environment on the planet, given us the ability to imagine the future and to foresee the consequences of our everyday actions. You might think of the male and female brains working in concert as **one complete human brain** that happens to be contained in two separate containers.

John Gray's landmark book, *Men are from Mars, Women are from Venus*,[81] started a new popular examination of women's and men's roles in relationships. Since it was published, brain studies have continued to reveal the causes of many of the differences between women and men. Some of those differences can be troubling or embarrassing to discuss or taboo or ignored until they become the straws that break a relationship's back.

## The Orgasm Gap

*My wife only has sex with me for a purpose. Last night she used me to time an egg.* Rodney Dangerfield

One of the major, troubling, embarrassing, taboo and ignored differences is the difference between women's and men's orgasms. Their duration, the time required in foreplay, the blame, the lack of available information and the fear of not satisfying a partner make orgasms a major factor in lack of fulfillment in a relationship. One

---

[80] *Music Instinct: Science and Song*, a groundbreaking documentary directed by Elena Mannes, 2009. Scientists and musicians reveal surprising connections between music, the brain, the body and human evolution.

[81] Published in 1992. John Gray's Mars & Venus empire continues to explore the physical, psychological, cultural and hormonal differences that make partnership such a challenge.

study showed that 85 per cent of men said they had an orgasm in their most recent sexual event, while 64 per cent of women said so.[82] The difference was said to be due to poor communication. It must also have to do with women faking orgasm. We know that women put themselves under great pressure to show that their male partner has satisfied them, even at the expense of their own gratification.

Far too many women will not talk to their partners about the triggers they require to reach orgasm, and we believe that every woman's trigger is different. As we said earlier, for Donna, the trigger is the romance conjured up by the music and lyrics from the 40s and 50s – Frank Sinatra, Peggy Lee, Ella Fitzgerald, etc. What's important is that no partner can know what that trigger is without being told. And some women have never thought about it themselves, so have never been able to let their partners know how to satisfy them.

Feminine empathy means that if a woman is sharing a space with another living being, some part of her brain is occupied in her concern for that being's welfare. In the bedroom, that means that, in addition to her normal brain activity of hearing and sensing everything in the room, plus wondering what he would like for dinner, plus worrying about the million details of day-to-day life, she is also hyper-aware of her sex partner's welfare. She listens to his every breath, feels his movements and wonders if he's actually enjoying himself as much as she wants him to, and what she can do to help him.

---

[82] Herbenick, D., Reece, M., Sanders, S.A., Schick, V., Dodge, B., & Fortenberry, J.D. (2010). Sexual behavior in the United States: Results from a national probability sample of males and females ages 14 to 94. *Journal of Sexual Medicine, 7* (suppl 5), 255-265.

Somewhere in there is the question, "Should I fake an orgasm for him?" The anxiety and self-consciousness centers in her brain take much longer than his to quiet down, so that she can begin to concentrate on pleasure alone.[83] Her male partner, meanwhile, is deep inside his 'orgasm box', and although he is also aware of her, his real focus is probably on his own pleasure.

## Boxes and Wire

We think that's one of the simple reasons why it takes most women so much longer to reach orgasm than most men. Women don't have an orgasm box. Their brain is built like a big ball of wire, as marriage therapist Mark Gungor says,[84] that is connected to everything, while men's brains are a series of boxes that are not allowed to touch. Men open one box at a time and focus on what's in the box. And they have a 'nothing box', which helps them recharge, and which we think is also the orgasm box.

Of course, that's not literally true, but it's a handy visualization of the brain differences. Men's brain activity is quite limited during sex and they need much less time to shut down the anxiety and self-consciousness centers in their brains. Studies show that different areas of the female brain are activated in orgasm, depending on whether a woman is alone or with a partner. The masturbatory orgasm excites 30 areas of the brain, so on a fMRI scan the brain is lit up, including parts of the pre-frontal cortex, the area involved in imagination and impulse-control.[85] In partnered orgasm, studies

---

[83] Louann Brizendine, *The Male Brain*, Three Rivers Press, 2010.

[84] Mark Gungor, *Laugh Your Way to a Better Marriage*. www.markgungor.com

[85] New Scientist, May 11 2011. Article on orgasm research at Rutgers University.

have shown that a woman's pre-frontal cortex shuts down, along with the areas that control fear and anxiety.[86]

## The Balance of Power

The natural balance of male and female cognitive power was altered by one-sided dominator cultures that forced their way into the Mediterranean areas where partnership cultures existed over six thousand years ago.[87] Male dominator tribes, with their cruel gods and passion for warfare, made women chattel and strove to force Nature into submission.

The suppression of the Feminine in partnership spread as men waging war became a dominant display behavior. The shift to imbalance within our species and a disconnection between us and the rest of Nature has continued to the present day, when our species has the ability to change weather patterns, wipe out entire species and reduce the planet to a smoldering wreck, should the men at the controls choose to do so.

Men have brains that can create great ideas and they may pursue those ideas with great focus and enthusiasm. The unintended consequences of those ideas might be devastating, but it is often the case that men will still carry on expanding on their ideas despite the damage being done. That's where the Feminine counterbalance comes in. Men can become stuck in their 'project box' because what they're doing is so interesting to them.

Discovering the power of splitting the atom was cool stuff. Dropping atom bombs, the Cold War arms race and the massive expansion of the Pentagon/CIA/NSA budgets were outcomes of that cool stuff.

---

[86] New Scientist, June 2005. Article on orgasm research at the University of Groningen.

[87] Riane Eisler, The Chalice and the Blade.

Finding solutions to pestilence and famine is a neat idea, but when corporate profits outweigh the effects of those solutions – such as the depletion of soils, the contamination of crops with genetically-modified strains that cannot reproduce, the poisoning of foods – then the men involved need to hear from the women in their lives that they are endangering future generations with their focus on 'progress', accumulation of wealth and continuing to try to bend Nature to our will.

The men involved in such projects, even if some of them have misgivings, quiet their doubts by quashing their own Feminine, and there are not enough Functional Female voices to whisper convincingly the message of reason and restraint.

That can change when each woman understands how men will adapt to the Functional Feminine when its concerns are made clear. From the bedroom to the boardroom to the Oval Office, men's brains are waiting for the balancing input from the female brain to give them a sense of purpose beyond just 'doing stuff'. Men make and do things partly as a display of their suitability as partners. Ideas dreamed up by the male brain become more satisfying when the female brain gives approval. It is a powerful guiding force.

It was the male and female brains as two halves of the one full human brain that made our species so successful at survival. As men's and women's roles in community diverged, so did their brain structures and the skills imparted. In the natural world, those two brains working together in partnership were the secret to survival. Then the Alpha-Mask Male societies began forming and cultures became lop-sided, more violent and less empathic.

The ongoing brain research explains so many of the difficulties that have made relationships so strained between women and men. The understanding of our differences is key to stopping the blame game and forming balanced partnerships at all levels.

# EPILOGUE

## Donna & Paul: Small Steps to Evolutionary Change

*Where Do We Go from Here?*

*Rather than inhabiting a top-down, command-and-control world, where those at the bottom have virtually no power, we are living in a highly interconnected world with changes rippling up and through billions of "nodes" – that's us and our communities.*
Frances Moore Lappé and Jeffrey Perkins, *You Have the Power*

So you've taken the first cautious step, taken another and another. Now you're in a long-term partnership of your own. What can you do to continue the shift that you have already started, with just these small steps, from patriarchy to partnership? It is a series of incremental advances that can be made by one person, whose example can be followed by another and another, until a social norm is created.

Here are some evolutionary changes and the small steps that can begin their implementation.

### Evolutionary Change: Kick the Habit

One critical part of moving from patriarchy to partnership is to give up the habit of blame. Although patriarchy means men have more control than women, it's not a man-by-man phenomenon. Men living now did not create patriarchy, they simply are going along with what they have been conditioned to believe. Men have to be shown that there are benefits in the shift to partnership, because they are afraid of change and the unknown, as are most people. We all like our routines, our comfort zones, the bubbles we create for ourselves. We need great inducements to change our habits. So it is with the status quo of our society, in which men have held sway for millennia. That's quite a habit to kick! So – NO BLAME! When you're trying to change someone's mind, it never helps to put them into defense-for-survival mode. We need to prove that there is a comfort zone that will feel and work even better than the existing paradigm.

### Small Step: Create Comfort

Make men comfortable in your company. Make your partner as comfortable at home as you would like to be. Make him amenable to respecting your opinions. Make him aware that your relationship takes two. Teach him gradually to think of your comfort as well as his own. Do not blame men for their inability to function naturally in relationship. They have to learn their skills from women. Whining is not an option, blame is destructive, the guidance of the Functional Feminine will make the most important, positive changes in his life.

### Evolutionary Change: Expose the Mask

The Alpha-Mask men who display the Dysfunctional Masculine traits of aggression and machismo may not understand that their need to do so stems from the biological, sexual display to women of their genetic strength. The display is exaggerated by their instinctive fear of rejection by women, as well as their inner knowledge of the act they are performing. Somewhere inside they know that they are not really the Alphas they want to appear to be.

To compensate they show a swaggering disregard for the damage they inflict on the people and the world. They feign indifference when they are rejected. They hide behind corporate and personal Masks to cut themselves off from any responsibility their real selves might claim. They socialize only with like-minded Alpha-Masks to further their self-righteous alienation from the common herd of humanity. Their Masks may become who they are, even in their own eyes. After all, they can only see the reflection of the Masks that they project.

The powerful Alpha-Mask men that carry on this destructive charade surround themselves with compliant underlings and trophy wives or Beta women from lower socio-economic levels, so that they can continue to be the big fish in their pond. Some of the Alpha-Mask men from other parts of the social scale act out their frustration at their powerlessness in society through violence and destructive behavior.

These are the torchbearers for patriarchy, actively participating in supporting it. Because they play the Alpha role, much of the rest of the male population tries to emulate them, compensating for their own lack of natural authority with aggression and callousness. As that becomes more normal, most men (and, it must be said, most women) simply go along with the cultural norms without giving them a second thought, preserving patriarchy by proxy.

It is that apathy that can be reversed when we become aware that there are possibilities beyond patriarchy and rampant machismo. As with most things, the change begins with the individual.

## Small Step: DO Talk to Strangers

When men think of other people, especially women, as The Others, they are really manifesting their inability to communicate. That's why Alpha male corporate executives are being trained to empathize and communicate better with their subordinates, and give them lessons in team building. Other men, who simply conform to their version of patriarchal ideals of manliness - strong and silent, aggressive and competitive, afraid of rejection and of being revealed as a person with feelings – must rely on the insight of women to turn them into communicators. That can only happen when women are ready to talk to them.

As women become less fearful of talking to men and with initiating contact with strangers, so men will become more accustomed to being talked to by women. Women, put yourselves in your nurturing mode, just as you do when you look at a baby or even a cuddly pet. By tapping into that and simply being friendly, these men will respond to your kindness. You make them feel real and noticed. Remember, their greatest fear is rejection.

From that point men will begin to expect to be contacted by women, and so the change will slowly take place, to the point where men accept that the initial approach and the subsequent contacts CAN be made by women. The small step is for women to be more willing to talk to strangers, both men and women, to create a more open and trusting public environment in which Male Masks have less power and can be lowered more readily. It's too easy for us to shut ourselves off and feel alienated and rejected by a silent society. It makes us more fearful of one another.

Talk to the checkout clerk; not just a "Have a nice day" but something a little less generic. Donna has fun with saying, "Have a nice life!" which always brings a smile and wakes them up. Everyone is human and everyone needs contact. Our personal fortresses in which most women, especially urbanites, hide in fear of strangers are an extension of the Male Mask. Those defenses are all products of the patriarchal mindset that has created the suspicious and fearful atmosphere on which tyrants thrive.

## Evolutionary Change: Sharing Sexual Choices

Our society is more sexually overt than ever, yet ignorance and irresponsibility remain. As a nation, we expose our children to sexual images every day, yet most American parents don't want to teach them how to be responsibly sexual. Most young women today in the USA still get most of their information about sex from their peers and Internet porn sites. What a tragedy that this is still happening in our 'enlightened" age. It can only create an unhealthy snowballing effect of misinformation, fear and lifetimes unfulfilled.

One-third of American ninth-graders have had sex of some kind, most of the girls saying that they wanted to feel close to someone, it's just sex anyway.[88] Real sex education in our state schools is an election-losing issue for politicians, but teenage mothers are vilified. Talking about sex is 'dirty', yet we are all sexual beings and all need to learn how to cope with the urges and the consequences. Meanwhile, as our children stumble around making so many wrong choices, the porn industry makes billions of dollars a year.

Sex therapists know that a distressingly large number of women do not know where their clitoris is and that many more have never had an orgasm. Now the big drug companies are creating a huge campaign to convince women that there is a medical condition called "Female Sexual Dysfunction". The magic orgasm pill they're all looking for could be worth billions to them, so of course they prefer that women be less, not more, educated about sex.[89]

---

[88] *Girls and Sex*, Michelle Burford, *O Magazine*, November 2002.

[89] *Orgasm, Inc.* A film by Liz Canner on the search for the 'female Viagra' and how a new 'medical condition' is being created to market it.

### Small Step: Talk About It

If an adult couple cannot talk to each other about sex, they will create tensions that might doom their relationship. When lovemaking is disappointing for either partner, there is less incentive to initiate it. As with all interpersonal skills, discussion and mutual consent is key.

Talk to your partner about sex. Firstly, tell him when it feels right for you to make love. He's probably always ready, at least in the early stages. When you make love, tell him what you want him to do, what feels good. As we said earlier, every woman has her own trigger that turns her on, which probably has nothing to do with Hallmark cards, flowers and chocolates, and there's no way he can know it unless you tell him. That does NOT make you a slut! And you don't have to worry about him losing his erection. When the sex is better for you, it's also better for him, physically and psychologically.

This is something you do together to make each other feel good and to create a bond. This is both of you trying to make the other happy. If you're not happy with his lovemaking technique, gently let him know what you would rather have him do. The same goes for him. If he wants you to touch him or move a certain way, he should tell you. Otherwise your lovemaking may turn into a rote, mechanical session of him quickly getting his pleasure and you feeling cheated.

There is so much that partners can teach each other with a little care, forethought and education. Loving acceptance of each other's individual sexual preferences or each other's lack of knowledge can help overcome any problems and begin the search for real information, not the misinformation that pervades our culture and creates so much discrimination, misunderstanding and perversion.[90]

## Evolutionary Change: Conscious Pregnancy

Apart from incidents of rape and failure of contraceptives, there is no such thing as accidental pregnancy. There is lack of education, inattention to physical cycles, lack of self-esteem, macho insensitivity, disregard of consequences and ignorance of reality. A woman knows when she enters the fertile time of her monthly cycle, if she has been taught to recognize the physical signs.

A man that has been her partner for some time may be able to recognize them too, but probably not reliably. Nobody knows better than the woman does when pregnancy is possible and men are likely to be too unconscious to ask while in the throes of sex. Children born by default rather than by conscious decision are more likely to suffer abuse and emotional damage that is passed on to the next generation, according to the American Psychological Association. Pregnancy and childbirth must be a joint decision of partners, if they are both to be held responsible for the consequences.

## Small Step: Learn the Signs

As people enter and continue in a relationship, they naturally share aspects of their lives with each other. There is hardly a more important aspect to be shared than the fertility cycles of the woman partner. If partners are sexually active and if they expect to share responsibility for offspring, both ought to know when the likelihood of pregnancy is greater. Women, tell him when you are reaching ovulation. Show him what happens to your body when

---

[90] Riane Eisler, *Sacred Pleasure: Sex, Myth and the Politics of the Body*, HarperCollins, 1995.

you are fertile. This is not a secret for you to keep, unless you are actually trying to shanghai a man into parenthood. Men, ask her if it's safe to have sex. If you or she don't know if it's safe, wear a condom, then both of you should start a program of learning what her body does during all parts of her cycle.

### Evolutionary Change: Men Accept Women as Initiators

After thousands of years of men believing themselves to be in control, we can see where it's heading. It's time to rethink male and female roles in general, and their roles in the mating ritual in particular. We've been fighting our biology for too long. Now we're asking that men accept that women possess the natural abilities to choose their mates.

### Small Step: Women Saying Hello

Men can now watch for women's signs of interest, while women can assume the major pro-active role in the courtship process. It's a brave shift, but if we accept that the damage caused to men by female rejection encourages them to act out their violent fantasy of what real men should be, then it is an important change to make. It will improve everyone's self-esteem, allow men and women to enjoy life more, bring more people together and even help the housing shortage by combining households. From there it's a series of steps towards men happily relinquishing some of their power to women. Partnership is possible.

### Evolutionary Change: Ain't Gonna Study War No More

Mothers, grandmothers, great-grandmothers wives, aunts and sisters all have influence on the development of boys. It is the boys who are taught that it is an honorable thing to be trained to kill their own species and others, even for sport. And that is countenanced by the women in their lives, because "that's the way it is". Boys are more often told to go out and play unsupervised than girls, so they become accustomed to doing things their way, even if that way is destructive, overly aggressive or violent.

Perhaps it's time to look at that attitude and study where the urge to war originates and how we can curb the violent side of man's instinctive competitiveness. We know that male mammals are competitive in order to display their genetic prowess to females. But men can be aggressive and competitive without being violent or ruthless; sports and the rules that govern them are an example of that. Soccer teams shake hands after the game because the teams know they did their best to beat each other, but this was a competition, not a battle. No hard feelings. So where does overly aggressive behavior start that can lead men joyfully into war and can it be curbed?

## Small Step: Rites of Passage

Violent aggression often stems from childhood damage or the need for survival tactics while growing up. For some men, it becomes the only part of their lives in which they can be recognized as a leader. Young men, lured by the power of violence and money and by the family-style support a gang can provide, become mobsters and gangsters. They are taught discipline and hierarchy, obedience to their superiors, and how to use violence. In that way, gangs are similar to the military, which also gives support while teaching the use of deadly force against 'enemies'. All such organizations have rites of passage as the young recruit passes from civilian to member of the group.

Cruel rites of passage reinforce the violent tendencies in young men. Adolescent circumcision of boys as a rite of passage into manhood is even more damaging than circumcision of babies, which itself imprints violence and betrayal on the infant mind.[91] In military schools and camps and on college campuses, hazing rituals continue brutalize young men, preparing them to be brutal in turn. Every year, they die from being forced to drink too much, being beaten or exposed to cold too much. It's the spiraling display of power that has no feminine guidance to tell it when to stop.

It's time for new rites of passage for young men trying to find their way in the world that go beyond joining the Marines. The new rites could be designed to teach such ideals as service to others, strong character, trust in others and trustworthiness, disciplined behavior without the need to follow blindly, curiosity, responsibility, bravery without foolhardiness, concern for all beings, empathy and caring.

What about introducing school programs to enroll the Alpha-Mask bullies into a positive rite of passage? Finding the kind of rites of passage that are daring and dangerous enough to be challenging, yet which do not exclude the less physically able, and that are educational and supportive is the key to this small step.

Programs such as Boys to Men (boystomen.org), Young Men's Ultimate Weekend (ymuw.org) and the ManKind Project (mankindproject.org) are all doing great work in mentoring young men into channeling their strengths not to war, but for the service of humanity.

The old accepted vision of humans, especially men, as immutably warlike is now challenged by scholars.[92] Our endless cycle of wars is just a cultural habit that we have reinforced with the notion of

---

[91] Marilyn Milos RN, in a panel discussion for *Seduction Redefined*. She is the director of NOCIRC (the National Organization of Circumcision Information Resource Centers) www.nocirc.org

[92] Frans de Waal, *Our Inner Ape*. Berkley Publishing Group, 2005.

honor in killing and the glory of death as a way of giving to the community we call a nation.

Academia told us that we inherit our aggressive and warlike tendencies from chimpanzees, while another ape, also closely related to us, the bonobo was ignored. The bonobos are an egalitarian, matriarchal species who use more peaceful methods for survival. They use sex as the great mediator, creating pleasurable resolutions to possible conflict. Perhaps that's why they didn't appeal to academics, especially in Victorian times.

For most of our history as a species we have been community-building social animals. We value altruism and loving relationships. For hundreds of thousands of years, our species lived in egalitarian groups in which war was an extreme anomaly.[93] Even now, despite the obscene amounts of money spent on killing one another, the vast majority of us live peaceful lives in which we get along with our neighbors and form close-knit communities. We value the empathic Feminine in our humanity.

If mothers began to prize the Feminine in their boys as much as the Masculine, to recognize both sets of strengths as 'human' rather than male or female, we'd be less afraid of 'contaminating' our sons,[94] there would be fewer Alpha-Mask males in the world and more Mindful Males. This may be the most important work of all for women.

---

[93] Douglas P. Fry, *Beyond War: The Human Potential for Peace*. Oxford University Press, 2007.

[94] Olga Silverstein, The Courage to Raise Good Men. Penguin, 1995. William Pollack, Real Boys: Rescuing Our Sons from the Myths of Boyhood. Owl Books, 1999. Dan Kindlon & Michael Thompson, Raising Cain: Protecting the Emotional Life of Boys. Ballantine Books, 2000

## Evolutionary Change: Stop Accepting the Status Quo

A major reason for the continuation of the habits of patriarchy in our time is the subtle propaganda-by-omission that is the norm in the news media. We accept what we are told when the war stories are about "people", rather than "men" and "women". We hear of "planes" bombing cities, of suicide bombers, and although we might visualize a man at the controls, without hearing it there is no immediate, conscious attention paid to the fact that a man is once again committing violence.

## Small Step: Genderize the News

We would like to hear the news being fully descriptive about the facts of war and violence. Instead of "planes", we want to hear "male (or female) pilots"; instead of "armed robber" we want to hear "male robber"; instead of "casualties" we want to hear the numbers of women, children and men that are injured. As we've stated repeatedly throughout this book, this is not about blaming men for their violence, it is a device to jar our brains into listening to the real facts – that men are doing most of the killing and dying, and that's because they have no-one to tell them when to stop.

## In Conclusion

Is it realistic to ask women to resume their position as the 'umpire' of civilization? Let's put it this way – without the leverage women possess naturally, the leverage of sexual selection, civilization wouldn't exist, because men would have had no incentive to create it for them. Without the comfort and safety women can provide, our civilization would falter. Without the nurturing and organizational power of women, there would be no incentive for men to stay with them and their offspring. Without the tenderness, wisdom and emotional strength of women, men would spend even more time than they already do in destructive and violent habits and shutting down the emotions that connect them to the rest of the world.

Is it fair that women play such a huge role in civilized society? It is their nature. Is it fair that they should have had to stand by and watch as men engage in degrading the civilizations it took so long to create? No. But men will not think about stopping until women show them another way. We are calling on women to remember and develop their Functional Feminine, so that they can join in encouraging and guiding the Functional Masculine in all the men in their lives.

Geoffrey Miller said this, "In America, the majority of men supported the Iraq War and the majority of women did not. That means there were a lot of mismatched couples. In those couples, were the women able to assert themselves, or did they stay silent, complicit; didn't want to make waves? I think both sexes have a moral imperative to realize that their own ideological decisions can affect society very powerfully, regarding the sexual choices they make and how they behave in an intimate relationship. It's the height of hypocrisy to say, "I am a peace activist, but I still love my husband even though he supports the war." That's where the leverage is - within the relationship. Women are in the driver's seat, where they can lead their husbands, boyfriends, friends."[95]

You don't have to be walking on the moon to take a giant leap for humankind. It can and must be done here on our groaning planet, while we still have a chance to survive. Small steps, giant leaps—both start with the will to take them. Women around the world may not have the political or social clout that men have, but they have the biological clout, and that is much more powerful in the long run.

---

[95] In an interview for Baring Witness. BaringWitnessFilm.org

## Seduction Redefined

With the will to exert that sensual power of the Functional Feminine, women can again be a force for species-wide evolutionary change. Their innate strengths combined with the Functional Masculine in the Beta Male majority and the Alpha minority will enable our species to break out of the Alpha-Mask dominator cultures that threaten us all. This is the time when change must and can happen before the runaway displays of Alpha-Mask violence and destruction go beyond the point of redemption.

It must begin in the western cultures, because we have more of the worst weapons and are desperate to maintain our unsustainable comforts at any cost to the world and all its life forms. We are emulated by the developing countries that see the luxuries we have and of course covet them, even as their environments and people are endangered by our search for cheap resources.

So what may begin with a woman being inspired to seduce a man into true partnership can become a template for the partnership of the Functional Feminine and Masculine in the world at large, starting right here.

*The world will be saved by the western woman.*
The Dalai Lama, 2009

# ABOUT THE AUTHORS

Scott Hess Photography

**Donna Oehm Sheehan,** a Northern California native and world traveler, is an artist, community/environmental visionary activist and Evolutionary Behaviorist. She has received state and national awards, including an AVA (Award for Vision and Achievement) for her inspiration behind the global anti-war organization, Baring Witness (www.BaringWitness.org), an Environmental Action Committee Steward of the Land Award, and a Giraffe Award (www.giraffe.org) for "sticking her neck out" in her work on pesticide reform with Mow&Sow (www.mowandsow.org), which she founded. She has twenty years of experience in researching and organizing. She co-founded a community radio station (www.KWMR.org) in Northern California and ORLO, an arts and ecology organization in Portland, Oregon.

Donna has conducted *Seduction Redefined* workshops, teaching women to give themselves permission to initiate courtship, build relationship and create partnership. Over eighty years old and in partnership with Paul, she feels successful, beautiful and sensual.

**Paul Reffell**, a world traveler and an English transplant to Northern California, is an Evolutionary Behaviorist activist who writes poetry, fiction, and non-fiction on Nature and human nature. He has performed his works on stage and on radio. He can also fix just about anything!

Since becoming partners and creative collaborators, **Donna & Paul** have worked together on many projects, including Baring Witness. They have co-written a book and personality profiling system that uses physical genetic indicators of left and right brain traits, called *BrainLines*, which can be seen at www.BrainLines.org. They have co-created interactive public art installations, *Wargasm* and *ProDegradation*, and this book, *Seduction Redefined*.

At present they are co-producing a feature-length documentary film combining Baring Witness and *Seduction Redefined* (*www.BaringWitnessFilm.org*). As part of their Evolutionary Revolution, they created the *Dolley Madison Partnership Award* (more information at www.DolleyMadisonPartnershipAward.org)

to honor couples in which the Functional Masculine and Functional Feminine have combined for the benefit of the world. They have been interviewed and featured internationally on TV, radio and in films.

Some of their current work can be seen at:

www.SeductionRedefined.com
www.BaringWitness.org
www.BaringWitnessFilm.org
www.MowandSow.org
www.BrainLines.com

# INDEX

Adam & Eve, xi, xii, xiii, xiv, xv, xvi, xvii, 136
*Agape*, 22, 129, 137, 146
Alpha Female, 9, 12, 14, 15, 16, 50, 147, 164
Alpha Male, 9, 12, 26, 31, 147
Alpha Male Syndrome, 9
Alpha-Mask Female, 15
Alpha-Mask Male, 5, 9, 12, 13, 14, 15, 16, 18, 53, 179, 199, 202, 203, 210, 211, 214
Angier, Natalie, 20
Anima & Animus, xvi

Barash, David, 74
Baring Witness, ix, 49, 158, 213, 216
BaringWitnessFilm.org, 5, 49, 213, 216, 217
Beauty, 32, 72
Beta Female, 9, 10
Beta Male, 9, 10, 11, 88, 130, 164, 184, 214
Bevington, Alden, xvii, xix
Blaming, viii, 2, 16, 27, 31, 41, 60, 81, 117, 125, 126, 135, 159, 160, 163, 178, 195, 199, 202

Boys, 42, 43, 44, 47, 75, 89, 113, 208, 209, 211
Brain Science, vii, 2, 3, 26, 43, 44, 68, 90, 97, 135, 137, 139, 142, 148, 149, 170, 192, 193, 194, 195, 197, 198, 199, 212
Brizendine, Louann, 191, 192, 197
Buss, David M., 35, 52, 56, 63, 65, 124, 153

Call, The, x, 26, 31, 32
Circumcision, 210
Colombian women's protest, 37
Commitment, 40, 90, 114, 140
Creative collaboration, 158, 159
Cultural myths & mores, viii, 6, 30, 31, 74, 90, 92, 116, 170, 181, 185, 187, 207

Dalai Lama, The, 214
Daly, Mary, 47
Dangerfield, Rodney, 153, 195
Darwin, Charles, ii, ix, xix, 23, 2, 17, 28, 33, 51, 52, 54, 61, 64, 73
Dates and dating, 84, 182
de Waal, Frans, 210
Dear Donna letter, 120

Deida, David, 109
*Descent of Man, The*, 23, 51, 52, 64, 73
Display, x, 2, 6, 7, 38, 52, 53, 59, 64, 65, 68, 146, 178, 184, 214
Dysfunctional Feminine, 20, 22
Dysfunctional Masculine, 20, 21, 22, 48, 202

Eisler, Riane, i, 36, 198, 207
Eldergasm, 168, 169
*Eros*, 22, 29, 129, 136, 146
Evolution, 17, 20

Fisher, Helen, ii
Fry, Douglas P., 211
Functional Feminine, 19, 21, 22, 47, 48, 179, 199, 202, 213, 214, 217
Functional Masculine, 19, 21, 32, 53, 213, 214, 217

Genderizing, 212
Girls, 42, 47, 72, 83, 89, 205, 209
Gottman, John, 143
Gowaty, Patricia, 52
Greene, Robert, 25, 95
Gungor, Mark, 197

Haselton, Martie G., 35, 124
Hrdy, Sarah Blaffer, 52, 74, 152
Hunting, 62

Initiating, 69, 87
Intuition, 27, 29

Kindlon, Dan, 42, 211
Kindness, 19, 56, 63
Knight in Shining Armor, viii, 26
Knowledge, iii, 31, 68, 88, 113, 118, 142, 151, 152, 187, 192, 203, 206

Lafrinere, Dorothy, ii
Lawlor, Robert, 36
Lerner, Gerda, 65
Liberian women's protest, 36
Love, x, 32, 41, 43, 121, 129, 131, 138, 139, 140, 143, 157
Loye, David, 51, 54
Lysistrata, i, iii, 37

Mackenzie, Margaret, ii
Maines, Rachel, 152
Male Mask, 8, 13, 15, 42, 44, 45, 46, 47, 60, 61, 65, 67, 70, 75, 87, 89, 90, 98, 112, 115, 116, 118, 138, 146, 151, 156, 173, 174, 179, 204
Male Mask List, 112
Manipulation, 101
Marriage, 31, 41, 44, 59, 87, 88, 96, 99, 111, 117, 125, 137, 143, 145, 153, 156, 161, 163, 172, 183, 184, 197
Matriarchy, 37, 155, 211
McNeil, Carmen, 43
Mead, Margaret, i
Meade, Michael, xvi
Medlock, Ann, iii
Men are more afraid..., 81, 82, 84, 89
Miller, Geoffrey, i, xix, 5, 49, 52, 62, 63, 72, 130, 141, 145, 178, 213
Mindful Male, 7, 11, 12, 18, 31, 211

Nigerian women's protest, 36
No strings attached, 26, 27, 40, 90, 126, 164, 182
Now, The, 122, 133, 166

Orgasm, 152, 170, 187, 195, 205
Osman, Lesley, ii

# Index

Partnership, i, ii, vii, ix, x, 1, 2, 3, 4, 8, 10, 11, 15, 18, 22, 27, 28, 31, 32, 33, 36, 37, 38, 41, 46, 47, 48, 51, 57, 60, 61, 68, 74, 76, 77, 90, 94, 99, 104, 105, 107, 108, 112, 115, 117, 129, 130, 135, 141, 142, 143, 144, 147, 151, 154, 155, 156, 157, 158, 159, 161, 163, 166, 167, 168, 172, 175, 177, 178, 179, 195, 198, 199, 201, 202, 208, 214, 216
Patriarchy, 14, 16, 46, 47, 65, 66, 204, 205
Peace, x, 211
Phillips, Tim, 63
Pregnancy, 207

Rejection, fear of, 89
Religion, 30, 31, 61, 117
Rifkin, Jeremy, 67
Robertson, Sarah, 28, 73
Ruigrok, Alina, 172, 173, 175
*Rules, The*, ii, 31, 56, 97
Runaway traits, 6, 7, 53, 55, 64, 68, 214
Ryan, Christopher, 74

Saad, Gad, 35
Sapolsky, Robert, 55
Scherer,, John, ii, 125
Segell, Michael, 47, 59
Serial Monogamy, 74
Sexual orientations, 3, 43, 51, 69, 97, 123
Sexual Selection theory, ii, ix, 23, 2, 10, 28, 33, 52, 53, 61, 64
Shlain, Leonard, 72, 87
Silverstein, Olga, 211
Sokol, Rosemary, ii
Sperm choice, 20
Spriggs, William, ii
Starr-Karlin, Larry, ii
Sueur, Jérôme, 64
Sunday Sex, 74, 117, 144, 145, 168, 169

Thatcher, Margaret, 15
The egg knows..., 20, 28, 29, 73

Vandermassen, Griet, iii, 53

War, 5, 158, 198, 208, 211, 213
Weinberg, George, 119, 149, 172
Wilson, David Sloan, 17

www.ingramcontent.com/pod-product-compliance
Lightning Source LLC
Chambersburg PA
CBHW060505090426
42735CB00011B/2117